The Napkin Approach

The Napkin Approach

◆

(the initial assemblage)

composed by shen brevard

iUniverse, Inc.
New York Lincoln Shanghai

The Napkin Approach
(the initial assemblage)

Copyright © 2005 by Shentale Brevard Randall

All rights reserved. No part of this book may be used or reproduced by any means, graphic, electronic, or mechanical, including photocopying, recording, taping or by any information storage retrieval system without the written permission of the publisher except in the case of brief quotations embodied in critical articles and reviews.

iUniverse books may be ordered through booksellers or by contacting:

iUniverse
2021 Pine Lake Road, Suite 100
Lincoln, NE 68512
www.iuniverse.com
1-800-Authors (1-800-288-4677)

ISBN-13: 978-0-595-37185-3 (pbk)
ISBN-13: 978-0-595-81584-5 (ebk)
ISBN-10: 0-595-37185-X (pbk)
ISBN-10: 0-595-81584-7 (ebk)

Printed in the United States of America

Contents

The Napkin Approach (the acknowledgment). 1

Hangover in Sunnyside. 3

Why I court celibacy, can nuns drive Mustangs? 8

Saying Good-bye to the band 12

5 Hours to Sunrise 15

Sorta 32 questions on a cold winter's day 38

Sick-n-Single (the breakdown) 40

Inspired by HPL while pondering JPL 61

Perdido in Flux (the quest) 63

Bitter Thefts of Happiness 65

Random Ring 68

Mendicant Exceptionelle (psalmody) 72

Blue Bay Arean Bye-Cha. 78

Notes and Bibliography. 83

Annie Laura Brevard
(the maternal grandmother)

Andrea Michelle Booker
(the ever cool sibling sister)

The former for allegorically financing my future by instilling within me the joy of literature and travel while striving for a certain sophistication.

The latter for financing (literally) the following literary accomplishment and never mistaking my dream for a self-deluding illusion.

AND SO...

Like life—sometimes—nowhere is the best "where" to be. No conclusion. No solution. Standing by while the multitude of every day instances are enveloped by the safe *Gray Area* (and its elixir deluding comfort zone). The just is. Solitude world of you. Yet, living is too exquisite to be rendered mundane or worse, kept in a teasing, dismal stagnation.

This scripted collage exemplifies modern society and its loose, oblique entrapment upon humanity and our true core essence. There will be static. Friction is to be encountered. Continuity cannot be induced.

Current events place this world along with its inhabitants—mainly—(albeit frustratingly) positioned on the fringe of a realm of transformation where those ubiquitous moments of uncertainty and despair, if left uninhibited—per chance evolve into a rush of endless tranquility.

Consider the following piece a reflective exploration into a free fall of intellectual adventure. Initially put forth by a single individual, this literary effort can easily be assessed and interpreted through your own analysis based entirely within the reader's acute or indiscriminate perception.

Even though we are as individual as a thumbprint—standing alone yet united in tone—it's all about the experience.

Enjoy. Happy thinking.

-shen

"Man is asleep. He has no permanent I, no real consciousness, no will. He is a helpless puppet in the hands of outside forces. He is a being that Nature has only half created. If he wishes to be complete he must complete himself.

"But this is the one thing that he refuses to do."

P.D. Ouspensky

The Napkin Approach (the acknowledgment)

◆

*shen brevard
Los Angeles summer 1998*

If this were a perfect world then there would be no God. There would be no need. Everything would be just so. However, if perfect were just an adjective and could be placed with any other adjective, then perfection would be either good or bad. The state of existence could go either way.

My world: the individual space encompassing you, your "loved" ones (a.k.a. family members, both immediate and otherwise) and associates, who also go by as friends, work mates and school mates. This immediate area surrounding you is only a small piece of the big picture of everything that nature encompasses—both seen and unseen. The world. Society…

Life is like perfection only the flaws tend to steer it into the neighborhood of the despondent, depressed and distressed. Therefore, one's existence can be perfect but, as in a perfectly disturbing manner. There are laws though that must always be adhered to in order for life to keep perpetuating. Balance is required. Yin for yang. Maat to counter Maati. Abandonment to challenge acceptance.

Is living or continuing in a sad way really existing? Does life itself have a "perfect" side even while it dwells in the throes of the negative? The various depths of depression is like a direct reflection on the life outside each of our own unique and individual worlds. Assistance, as in man-made and as in man himself, can be used to uplift those who have fallen into various degrees of negativity. Viewing and experiencing joy, peace or what can pass for happiness is really only temporary. Existing is ongoing but, how it's done or performed is what places it in constant flux.

Can another human being provide relief from a qualifying state of anguish? Is the mental joining of two, to form one, as in a relationship between a man and a woman, the key to attaining and sustaining harmony?

His smile and actions were all that had been needed to solidify the belief that perhaps the ongoing down mood of mine was about to enter a cycle of serenity aided by his presence. This assumption was cut short—extinguished in the premature stage of development. The visits and dates devolved from eagerly making time to abruptly stopping. Sporadic yet steady phone calls dropped to scarce then nil. Loneliness ensued and a big, empty want was born.

Now, in a bar but, really it could be anywhere, as long as spirits and bottles containing spirits, surround my aging melancholy—I stare at the empty glass with the half melted ice cubes inside. I remove it from my sight then begin to study the white, square shaped napkin which remains. It is a perfect square. I extract a pen from my purse and jot:

"Here is a napkin. Not much to some, but a lot, at this moment, to me. Perhaps it can help end my agonizing situation? It can communicate to you what I cannot. So, hear the napkin's words. I miss you and am sincere. Do you even care? Did you ever care? After one drink most are on their way to saying way too much. Me, I take the opposite path and say very little. But, the napkin is waiting and so am I."

Finished, I stand, walk over to him and his "date" and lay the perfect white napkin, containing my freshly inked thoughts, in front of him. During the interval that it takes for him to realize me, the note and what is occurring, I feel nothing. I am numb with anticipation. Yet a piece of me simply desires to curl up into a ball and instantly disappear. If life ended as I know it and there is an "other" side, God just might be there. However, what form of perfect is that?

Hangover in Sunnyside

♦

shen brevard
Brooklyn spring 1998

I used to think the more you drink, the more brain cells you kill. My hopes were, and still are, that the memory cells will be the first to fade. Memory, as in people, especially concerning significant others and would-be significant others. Alcoholic beverages would be my convenient and fast road to serene bliss. Since love, passion and desire avidly shun me, my own peace with happiness can solely be attained through memory loss and a personalized style of hypnotherapy.

Writing used to provide a temporary sanctuary from all the gloom and mediocrity of my life. Now, my mind is too beaten and exhausted to create even a dangling modifier—much less a sentence. When one desires to write, to create, to dream of another world, obstacles come into existence as if the ancient gods themselves decreed a treacherous and perilous path to be trod. Surviving a dry spell in writing is one thing but, trying to overcome a bland and hopelessly tepid love life is another. When the two descriptions above are coupled with an unsteady income, barren is the only word deftly describing the situation.

It doesn't matter if one is a man or woman where emotional emptiness is concerned. Right now, all I can confirm is my feeling heart exists in the realm of somber ineptitude. I exit the building where I had spent the night and wander aimlessly into the weak light of the summer sun. It is late afternoon and overcast. I stifle a cynical snicker as I believe the weather is even cliche-ish regarding my mood.

I had the opportunity to wake earlier. However, when my former work associate left, my eyes couldn't bring myself to see them as they departed for a place where I should be, but didn't belong anymore. The subway stop is a few feet away. Entering the gate and ascending the old, dirty cement stairs which lead to the platform, my movements possess a fluidic sluggishness.

My mind sidetracks to imagine who else has walked these very same steps throughout the history of Sunnyside. The slightly dry, chapping lips attempt a small smile and are met with a wooden reception. My entire head is like a leaden piece of hardening cement. Any effort to divert it from normal functions is punished by a searing pang of anguish. I allow the cooling and stick to visual activities.

A few other individuals appear to be patiently waiting. I slump down on a bench and try to maintain a straight posture. Not that anyone here cares. Not that I really care. The raggedness of their attire along with clinging solemn anger composing their expressions, leads me to believe they too are grappling with personal setbacks such as myself. Poverty seems to be the very trend in the air. The oh so dry but very entertaining British author, Charles Dickens himself, eluded to the fact that lack of money and possessions coupled with an undercurrent of hopelessness could very likely lead to the abuse of alcohol.

A single token for the subway along with an invalid Metro card with nothing else occupies my jean pockets. My job with a big and downright commonly evil corporation had come to an abrupt end less than 24 hours ago. I was already living below paycheck to paycheck. This new added description, no incoming funds, seemed so horrid I couldn't dedicate any thought toward it. Being fired is a first for me. Being depressed is like returning home to an old, nagging relative. A work acquaintance whom had just recently escalated to the role of drinking partner, attempted to ease the subtle shock of my new found unemployed status by inviting me to their home. That was where I had just departed.

After entering the building yesterday, everything, all of my activities from that point on, were nothing but a blur. Dickens comes to mind yet again. The almost insatiable thirst inhabiting my throat brings me back to the seemingly endless amounts of wine and cocktails eagerly ingested the night before. My humanity is steadily slipping away as my personality is blossoming into a lemming-like creature. As far as the new lemming-like me is concerned, all self-control—whether involving food, liquor or just life in general—is nonexistent. My very foundation of feelings possesses an uncontrollable and unstoppable *munch* quality.

My limits are in the neighborhood where shame and humility—and respect for that matter—do not reside. Every aspect of my existence is becoming excessive. If I were an artist, and not just a wannabe aspiring talent, I could just attribute everything to the tortured, self-destruction that dwells in most artistic souls. But, the extent of my true creative talent was spent long ago on piano lessons and dance classes my ever hopeful parents forced me to attend, until I was old enough to convince them their money should be invested in more enterprising prospects.

The train arrives. I board along with the other bleak individuals. The subway car is sparse where people are concerned so, once again all are left to their own personal ponderings without any disturbance stemming from forced social interaction. The ride into the city is shorter than I remember. I transfer at a large station where more people are milling about with the ever present glum expression. The fact that everyone seems to match my melancholy mood is becoming eerily disturbing. Quickly, I find the designated platform for the train which will take me home. I sigh heavily as I expect a long wait.

As long as I have been alive and cognizant of my surroundings, the R train seemed to be the most infrequent of the subway system. The only other line to give it any competition is the N. I had subsequently dubbed them the Never and the Rarely. (1) Unlike before—back in Sunnyside, Queens—no one is waiting for my train, the Rarely. I look across the tracks and wince a bit as an express noisily passes. Somewhere imbedded deep within the recesses of my mind, I wonder if H.P. Lovecraft, the great gifted writer, ever had to withstand such obnoxious aural ruckus. An inner chuckle emerges as I reflect upon the fact that Mr. Lovecraft was never 'hung-over' per se since he was an ardent teetotaler and happen to rabidly despise those who consumed alcohol. For some reason, I am reminded of my dying brain cells which were attacked by the liquor the night before. Self disgust paired with deep regret aptly describes my present persona. To my surprise, I peer down the tracks for my train and the Rarely is making an appearance.

I board. More people are in this car than the last. It doesn't bother me since I am still able to attain a seat to myself. As I court my solitude, my eyes can't help but observe the others in the car. A man who appears to be my age is sitting directly across from me. He is reading Virgil's *The Aeneid*. While attending college, I had discovered Virgil in the library late one night while cramming for a Poli-Sci exam.

The tale of betrayal in love which evolved into the undoing of a nation provided more intrigue than learning the workings of the American political structure. I failed the final but, found an exquisite and now favorite epic story. I ease a bit more back into the hard, subway seat. My mind conjures up a vision of the Wailing Fields—the site of the last encounter between the Trojan war veteran Aeneas and betrayed Carthaginian leader Queen Dido. As the subway car swerves left then right, I wonder what was going through the mind of Aeneas as he witnessed with his very own eyes what his abandonment had wrought. How did he feel knowing his abrupt exit had rendered the once glorious Queen into a numbing state of catatonic longing?

The Wailing Fields were located in a subdivision of Tartarus. Tartarus was either lower than Hell or Hell itself. I can't quite remember and frown as I allow my eyes to look elsewhere. A young couple, most likely around my age, are seated three seats away. The male is eagerly whispering into the ear of the female. She in turn giggles. Actually, I can't hear his words or her giggles since the Rarely we are on has extra squeaky wheels. The peace and enjoyment both their faces harbor, lead me to ascertain theirs is a new love. Fresh and young and as of yet unmarred by mistrust, lies and heated arguments. Not that their union would ever mature to that. However, the state of society, of people in my age range and beyond these days, seem to follow a guideline where promises are easily made only to be quickly broken and discarded.

The train comes to a stop. I stand then nearly sprint off the Rarely. It has become too much. My thoughts, the subway companions, the loss of the job, the underlying dread of life which is metaphorically reaching out to me ever since opening my eyes this afternoon. All make me feel small, insignificant and an overall non-contributor to modern day America. I fight back tears and am unsuccessful. The first ones cloud my vision just as I reach above ground. One of my hands automatically wipes them away and I'm able to locate a bar before more spring forth.

Today is Friday. Tomorrow is Saturday. The weekend is here and Monday will shortly follow. Thus, a new and uncharted emotional territory will be ushered in. The liquor is making it easier for my senses to understand and accept my unemployed status. Sometimes when one drinks it can go beyond missing time and prolonged blackouts. You reach a numb state of consciousness where reflection upon your past actions is dominant while simultaneously being underlined by a constant background filled with paranoia.

By the time I enter the bar, tears are freely flowing and my cheeks are very damp. One of my hands reaches for my wallet and absently shows my identification—while my body slides onto a barstool. The bartender nods and stands nonchalantly by as words try to form in my mouth to order the drink of my desire. What could I possibly have that might just allow me to reconnect with the rest of humanity? How had my day, my life become so mundane? I place an order and wonder if the stage which my existence has now entered is merely an interval between jobs. Or, if I am embarking upon a journey into failure, destitution and a new budding addiction to alcohol?

Why I court celibacy, can nuns drive Mustangs?

◆

shen brevard
San Francisco winter 1998

I am sitting in an offbeat, out of the way cafe when a bout of solemn melancholy sweeps over me and takes hold of my senses. The whiskey colored skies of the beautiful spring sunset is really only ushering in a desolate eve of another solitary weekend. What sits before me is a firm preamble of the next few days ahead. Notes, scribbled by my eager hand, graciously intermingle with books and biographies of men and women from eras when valor reigned. I'm not sure how many tomes sit before me—could be five or possibly seven. It's enough though to create a pile.

How strong. How secure. Their presence only fortifies my solitude. I would rather subject my senses to admirable *personas* of the past than to expose myself to the dangerous and hollow encounters of today, also known as, "dates." My ego—more like self-esteem—has been shredded so much over the past four years. I wonder why? I keep asking myself why shallow warrants more than depth.

In this time I'm too romantic. I'm nostalgic to the point of being dreadful. I'm useless in the present and not worthy of current "deprogramming." In other times, such as long ago and before (or maybe in what's to come), I'm more than appreciated. My existence is venerated.

Back to the now and the overwhelming sorrow, pity frustration and loneliness. I want so much to not feel, to not care. The only desire stirring inside me these days is to become immersed in academics. My mind, body and soul only desire to learn Latin. But, lack of funds is proving an adamant adversary in regards to my progress. If I become a nun though, I wonder if Latin would be offered free of charge? If so, the exchange would be no more men. Not that it matters. It's been since April of last year since I last kissed someone. It was Easter weekend. How symbolic. Perhaps the 25th of December or on the 31st of October as it slides into the 1st of November, will produce someone to kiss me once again?

Maybe before this is to occur, a great epiphany will take place and my fate will be revealed to me in one gloriously, splendid second. With my free Latin lessons in swing accompanied by a budding nun-hood intro, no longer will I need men. No longer will I crave flesh. Adieu reptilian brain and all the carnal cravings hibernating within your insides. Fuck the U.S.A. or is it forget these turbulent, twisted times? My eyes find the now rust tinted sky, coupled with the fading sunlight. A high altitude achieving lone jet-plane disappears just over the horizon.

When I exist beyond the border of this emotionally barren and borderline restrictive society, I have a choice. I have an ego. I am alive. I am appreciated. I am told so. Women need men need females need males. Students need classes requires life attains experience. My eyes return to the silent pile consisting of books and bios. What if I could contact some of these individuals? What if an open channel could be forged? First person to greet would be Laurent Kabila.

The manner in which he had been able to acquire enough funds to maintain an almost 35 year civil war is more than enough validation of his "proposition" prowess. Our correspondence will enable me to attain the skills ensuring a cash flow necessary at sustaining my yearning for a gloriously, (now) antiquated lifestyle. Kabila can amply instruct how to attain far off sponsors with very poor vision, or ones who harbor an indifferent attitude when it comes to their money. After finances are set, my adventurous side can prevail.

To dance with the rapidly fading, valiant "Infamous" such as Calixto Morales is one such hope. I can find an abandoned bulldozer any day, any hour, to combat racism. And, Bolivia, where it did not go so well for one whom really cared about many who only misunderstood him entirely. A car from nearby comes to a "screeching" halt. Thus end the daydreams.

The tomes remain though. No mere noise can eradicate them as swiftly as my silent aspirations had been. As I look over my notes intertwined with the bios, I realize some men you can kill. And, with them their entire existence is extinguished. However, with others, a special chosen few, a hope and dream and plan for a new way, a more improved life for all, perishes forever.

Tonight, I sense a good cry. My eyes shall shed tears not for my own selfish wants, not for my own carnal cries for desire. No. I will weep for the passing, the slaughter and utter disillusionment of the tortured good and the martyred young. Those who were sacrificed for the benefit of hoping their deaths would usher in an age of benevolent grace. News to you all from simple, little me: Jesus the Nazarene tried and now tell me, after looking at recent events—did he succeed? (It was his ideal (wish) not to be idolized.) Or, has man triumphed in championing his "true" cause. Without some form of acknowledgment that you are desirable, wanted, needed, necessary, one is rendered into feeling like nothing.

Yourself, your psyche diminishes into a thick void of unworthiness. Authentic caring people are replaced by the foolishly happy and easily contented inauthentic. Does anyone even know about the Kashmiri sapphire and its exquisite reality anymore? (2) Confirmed precious gem, neglected oh so eagerly. This obscure and complex dichotomy of the extreme is enough to crush and defeat the strongest of wills. To destroy the most determined, passionate souls requires only a novice touch when someone operates (maneuvers) within the realm of a society like the modern U.S. One can only ponder for so long before tiring of the stagnating cycle of frustration. Bitterness can no longer quell the sting of "not wanted-ness." "Nothing" becomes a void dwelling in an emptiness ten times greater than a mature, distant black hole.

Being told you're something and someone who must and will perform some task exists on the opposite side of the knowing yourself and your capability spectrum. I finish my coffee. My big, bowl cup brings me back to the days spent in other countries with other individuals where men not only looked but, acted upon their feelings concerning me. The coffee is tepid. My thoughts are beyond the point of a fresh recycle. And, my overall mood of wait and anticipate is so unappealing.

The carnal me is quickly advancing and easily engulfing my ethereal abstraction. Perhaps I'll finally take heed of an American male's suggestion posed to me not long ago, "Shed 20 pounds. Get a breast job. Dumb down and lose some of the intensity when it comes to everyday life." Personally, I'd rather keep my passion, lose my desire for an intimate relationship and then strive for something more tangible than my recent, wishful imaginings—like drive a Mustang GT 'til my foot gets tired and my vision becomes a blur.

Saying Good-bye to the band

◆

shen brevard
Tokyo summer 2003

Can I not too connect in aloha and wish my fellow creators and aficionados of the craft a fine and fair adieu without the blunt cynicism and polite racism directed toward my 'sphere?' To them, the bland progenitors of this land, my sayoonara will always be seedy; something less than a genuine fan.

Always on the periphery of those who participate hito bito, people, in their minds, their miniscule space with humble arrogance abound, thinly secured (fastened) behind a façade of forced social grace. Who's the catalyst, whether in the Occident or the Orient? A dichotomous existence of a hi-tech society mired in 1950s Americana. I can't get with that. Or, Pax Robotica.

Yes Donald, *Where are we going*? And, Sarah, *How long has this* (truly) *been going on*? My senses have learned to absorb the cool, vapid glance of truth, the rude distinguishing factoid to recognize the brutality of the infamously persistent *isms* of modern man: whether elite, sex or race. Capitalizing on the ugliness of society and it's sophistication of decay; this trio of pessimism will never dissipate.

No matter where I go: Brooklyn to Paris, Marin to Malibu, Tangiers to Tokyo…Buy a ticket for travel on the TGV or the Shinkansen, it's really all the same. (3) While the vanguards of jazz cheer me on and fill me up with the ultimate optimism from a hip, nonphysical place…Here I am, here I stand just saying goodbye to the band. With a cool, complacent face, like Nina, *I'm Feelin' good*. Next stop, nonstop to Brasil.

Why stay to lament about a defunct love affair or a never existing freedom? For is something truly defunct that has actually never been?

"Consider depression (psychotic & chemical aside) an adventure into the deeper side of life."

Genevieve Paulson, *Kundalini and the Chakras*

5 Hours to Sunrise

◆

shen brevard
Los Angeles winter 2004

She has short, black hair, semi-slanted shaped eyes, a bow shaped mouth, is of average height (5'5 1/2 in reality, 5'6 otherwise) and body size. She is an aspiring writer.

"I no longer have a name. Why bother? If I view the world in description—basic adjectives—then why must I be any different? Writer-to-be, that's me."

A horn honks from the vehicle behind alerting her that traffic is beginning to pick up it's pace from solid standstill to moving parking lot. As her feet engage in a clutch, gas, brake dance, the aspiring writer's ears connect with a tune emanating from the car beside her.

"*I think I'm going outta my head over you…*"

"…la la la la la la…I wonder if the person who wrote those words realized the double entendre: Love or Looney? Desirous or Dangerous? Sensual or Stalker? Hmm…a triple entendre if that even exists."

The traffic stops all movement. The song fades then ends. She rolls up her window.

"Early evening chill no more. With gas prices mimicking a 'Carteresque' approach, heat should be generated by body and clothing. Odd and even plates here we come! Welcome back, Kotter. Now, there's a double entendre to occupy your brain."

She smiles. The aspiring writer zips her jacket closed.

"I am in control of my life but something else, some force is directing its course. And, the strangeness is the energy is emanating from deep within myself, my being—the very core of my psyche."

To distract herself, the aspiring writer turns on the radio. Her knob will not budge beyond an obscure a.m. station. No CDs are in sight so she surrenders her time to the on-air voice.

"…yeah, yeah, yeah and he will have a rap album and a rap sheet all in number one ratings by next week. Say it out loud Leon, they're Black and they're pro…"

"Uh..they are called African-American now, Dan."

"Yeah, well, African-American and proud, yo'. Hah, hah, hah."

She responds mentally.

"Racism. Goodness. Love it or leave it. Matter-of-fact, that grand ol' "ism" is on the rise; along with its eager associates sexism and excessive capitalism."

She ponders and frowns.

"Elitism never went away, though. It never truly does. That old stalwart—it's like rust, old Chevys or better still: Herpes. Wherever one looks, there they are. I've never possessed any of the above. Rust, well, figuratively speaking, permeates and "stagnates" the mechanization of society's propulsion into the better. For obvious reasons concerning the latter pair, Thank God! Regarding the former, I already have the "Death Mobile" no more patriotic purchasing—this life is already spoken for—addressing the latter.

A car zips by, followed by another then several more. They are exiting. The young woman soon does the same.

"Hmm...moving. Cars, yeah. Domicile, wow. U.S.A. really relieved. Asia's nice to visit but to live..."

The aspiring writer has just ended a two year self-imposed stint in Asia. She taught English, saved some funds then returned back to what she knew. Southern California. Reflecting upon her recent transpacific move:

"God! What a solo adventure, pseudo-Jonny Quest-style. Only with the glaring absence of his best friend Hadji, Race Bannon and his scientist father, Dr. Benton Quest. Come to think of it, I could've used Race's quick thinking in attaining a fast resolution to all my recent "little fires.""

"International relocation stress, glad to see it gone—dissolving fast into the abyss of the near past. I know more will come to replace it soon. The near future. My problems are myriad, they never travel alone. More like in packs of "threes and twelves" (subtle hyenas of my mind). They shield themselves from resolution. Hah, wait, myriad rhymes with pyramid. Sorta.

"I always wondered if I'd see those before I die. But then again death may not be as final as many may think. Physical of course, yes. Spiritual, hmm...now there's a quagmire of concern. But, back to the pyramids."

She skillfully continues to maneuver her compact SUV through the night streets of Los Angeles, California.

"The closest was Vegas but, then that rings a bit cheap, false and superficial. Most of modern society's manmade objects are aptly described in such a way. Can't these people see?

"Or does pain and solitude free oneself from the mundane reality of the mediocre physical? When it really comes down to it, good and evil only exist on the superficial surface of reality. Nothing in this world is truly, thoroughly good. While nothing on this earth is genuinely evil. People tend to misconstrue situations and circumstances when they have to give up more than what they are comfortable with; they couple it with the almighty evil, *bad,* something of a malevolent nature. They'd rather stick to what they know and that which makes them feel okay. Comfortable so to speak. Disturbing one's comfort zone without providing a cushion (e.g. religion, sports, morals—as in what's *right* by current societal standards and what's *wrong*) well, one must expect the extremely unpredictable as the immediate result."

Just then a car cruises through a yellow light. A stopped vehicle eager to get the jump on the (just turned) green light, has the right of way yet, almost collides with the casual driver. The aspiring writer smirks.

"Sorta like that. Amber lighting through life until someone or more likely some *thing* puts a stop to all that motion. Bam! Commotion. Metal meets metal. Who wants to meddle in it? Most want to escape. Some call it laziness. I define it as mid-30's malaise. Or better stated, refugees from responsibility. Hmm…ponder ponder."

The semi-slanted eyes spot a bookstore. The aspiring writer adheres to an urge to pay homage to literature. The spacious parking lot provides an abundance in choice where parking is concerned. Once inside, a seat is attained and the aspiring writer sequesters herself onto it with a book in hand. A slight scuffle attracts her attention.

"Truly, it is indeed fascinating, or just sheer ingenious play performed by some unfortunately bored bookseller concerning the consistently close proximity of the horror and romance genres in most American bookstores." (4)

The noise had been caused by a person who was most likely an upper class suburban homemaker as she slightly bumped an individual who was most definitely a hard core Goth guy.

"When worlds collide. Hah. Johnny Jones is on his way, Janet, so you better watch your next step. Love to him is very unreal."

A silent snicker riffs the rim of her lips as she allows her mental imagery to take full control of her senses.

"He started with bugs and the proverbial magnifying glass. Then moved up to cats. Becky Johnson's Tabby was never, ever found. Now, he's ready to be a true CourTV-er. Look closely at his reading material then balk soundly at his personal prose. *They all had it fuckin' comin'!!!* Rah. Rah. Rah. Blah. Blah. Blah. Who is the one with a profound proclivity to paranoia?"

Abruptly, she ends the silent soliloquy and sits upright.

"Jeez, sometimes I wish I could shut my mind off."

Her ears are suddenly aware of music. It is another version of *I think I'm goin' outta my head*.

"I guess that's my cue to adios or actually, vamanos. Yo voy. Maybe that's my theme music? Ick. Why so direct, Jackson? I wish the Cosmic Masters would've chosen something a bit more innocuous like the theme to *The Smurfs*."

The cool night air is refreshing as she returns back to the now nocturnal L.A.

"Oop. Waitaminute. That's definitely serial killer music sounds if there ever was. I can even hear the voices that always make you do *it*. The *its* and *things* discussed freely on cheap debasing talk shows with a parent or bewildered guardian infinitely shouting, *When the hell did it all go wrong?* The great escape."

The aspiring writer slips into the automobile. The patriotic purchase: as she has so deftly deemed the death machine. A 2005 American brand yet Japanese designed vehicle with a litany of limitations.

Two heating core replacements, one collapsed axle, gas pedal that sticks, flashing (what she terms as "disco") dashboard lights, CD player on constant 'shuffle' mode, writing long 'love' letters to Fix Or Repair Daily, two Dispute Settlement Board conference calls ending with more stagnating inertia. To buy back? Or, to not buy back? The aspiring writer telling them, 'I'm gonna die in this vehicle and you're gonna kill me.'

"Doesn't take much to be a psychic these days."

Her fingers swiftly lock the doors. The delirious diatribe from before lingers and languishes in her mental conscience.

"The *it* deed. The *bad*. Hmm…ponder ponder."

She locates then slides *Jimmy Smith's Greatest Hits* into the CD player.

"C'mon, Monsieur Smith, I wanna walk on your wild side."

The vehicle is pointed towards the street. As she shifts into third gear, her thoughts do as well.

"Can't wait to receive those keys. Bungalow here I come! Just north of National, acceptably west of Robertson and semi-comfortably south of Pico—safe to say I fall squarely inside the cusp of cool."

Her stomach emits a low, quick growl.

"Perhaps I should grab some grub?"

The aspiring writer heads toward La Cienega. Always hearing about this particular establishment, the young semi-Hungered decides to treat herself amongst other Dots but, ones who are more affluent and influential than herself. After easily attaining a parking space....

"San Francisco eat your heart out!"

...she heads in the direction of the trendy, posh restaurant. A loose, chic shawl (acquired in New York City's garment district) drapes her unsure shoulders. In line, she sizes up the other, super cool patrons by their dress, mannerism and snooty looks.

"Funny how a slightly more abundant bank account seems to empower individuals. And, when it comes to Dots that empowerment leads to "Caesar and Caesarina status." Most look like they ride horses or at least own a few. Here I stand on La Cienega. Waiting, waiting to get inside a restaurant. But, is that all? Am I trying to forge or pry my way into more than just a dining establishment?"

The inquisitive eyes spy a few soon-to-be diners eyeing her in a disapproving manner.

"Could it be my attire? Lack of attitude? Or, barely there assets? These people are really actually harmless. Sticks and stones, Jones, no broken bones. Simple, basic respect between fellow man is but a mere figment of the average and above average imagination. Navigating Drake Passage in a homemade canoe would be a task easier accomplished. Hola, Tierra del Fuego. G'day to ya, Cape Horn. Angle right onto Antarctica."

She huffs out of frustration and exasperation and decides to leave the line. In the blind acceptance of what must transpire—her leaving—the aspiring writer inadvertently brushes against several people. Mentally, her words play out.

"Hell, I just want to move on. Progress. Go forward in creation at a higher elevation. To tap into an inner plane which will institute magnanimous change from the interstitial level to the outermost aura. Third Dimension dwelling is so densely dull. And, most certainly indelectable."

The young woman locates the death-mobile and is soon safely inside. Back in the driver's seat the aspiring writer maps out a plan.

"I don't want to go too far. Even though I have plenty of time before storage opens, five hours can seem deceptively too long and sinisterly too short."

She flashes back onto several nights before. Avoiding the human noise machine, a.k.a. the loud, rude-n-crude roommate, she had driven out to Angeles Forest. It was dark, cold windy and the park was closed due to either budget cuts or it being off season and budget cuts. The ride back had been a sheer hellacious challenge.

"This here is stick driving. If I make it through this night, and off the Grapevine, I will have a T-shirt made, *I survived the qualifying rounds for the Gorman Grand Prix*. That is the only thing bringing any sense to these asinine fast driving fools. Clear skies = fast, roll. Clouds in sky, serious wind and rain to boot = not fast, slow roll. Didn't you get the memo, you illiterate bastards?

"I'm glad I voted to put more cops on the streets. I hope CHP is generously embellished."

A car, as if on cue, whizzes by the aspiring writer. It's generated wake turbulence causes her vehicle to slightly swerve.

"Yeah. One of those new cops needs to come and arrest his ass—set some examples—instate some seriously, structured, societal order—Japanese style."

The wind shakes her auto as if in agreement.

"My God! Isn't he even effected by the wind? This is beyond the Santa Ana, look at all those tumbleweeds. I can't stand it, Bandit."

Her flashback ends with a weak smile and semi-fatigued decided destination.

"More 70s references, even in recent flashbacks."

The aspiring writer has returned her consciousness to the Now. Behind the wheel of her parked car. Sitting mired in anticipatory angst.

"Was I so pensively peculiar to their eyes? Probably thought I was insane. *How dare that shabby, odd outsider attempt a squeeze in*! Not a card-carrying member of the pure desideratum of 21st Century mankind. Hmm…ponder ponder."

She could read but, her eyes are too tired and there's not enough light. A memory, audio only, is recalled. 'You actually still read books? But, you graduated from college ten years ago. You're not in school no more.' It had been the voice of a coworker.

"They are the Norma Desmonds of the world. Who needs words when we all have eyes blocking out the unpleasant, bad and brutal and beautiful? Hmm…the eyes in the hills, Papa Jupiter. Fear that. Not this. Hah. I know."

The aspiring writer points the death mobile in the direction of Sunset Boulevard. Her intended destination is not the flashy nightlife side. She's proceeding towards the beach, where the Norma Desmonds just might still linger in order to espouse inspiration.

"Modern 'Haters of words' aren't as depth possessed as their counterparts of the past. No. They are just your average Bullshilinos and Bullshilinas."

A sigh escapes the bow shaped lips.

"Theme music is engaged."

Wes Montgomery's *Bumpin' on Sunset* (5) eases into the interior of the passenger compartment. If she would have chosen the other side of Sunset, the young woman's music would have been vastly different.

"Ahh, *Sunset People*. Donna Summer. The 70's again. Night after night. Doin' it right. What's with that era? First Carter-n-Kotter, Disco-n-Smokey and the Bandit, now Donna, who's next? Oh but, Wes, please forgive me. You're from an entirely different epoch. Like the season of the superb. Please excuse me as I bask in *The Shadow of your Smile*."

The slow, hypnotic thump of the 50s/60s genre song takes over and nulls all thoughts for the duration of the Sunset Boulevard romp.

"Can you help me with my mind? Set it straight and ahead."

Another track begins.

"No way, Jose!"

It's *I think I'm goin' outta my head*. Instrumental but, recognizable.

"I totally forgot Wes recorded this tune. What a kick! Or a kill? Reminder of the obscure signs of where one's mind dwells. For it's the noises lurking behind the noises which individuals must heed. Or, is it words behind THE words? Maybe it's the words generating the noises in between sound? The frequency of life or the pitch of death."

Although a segue cannot be found after her Sunset Boulevard swing by, she back tracks down (then diverts off) the famed street where the aspiring writer finds herself in a what she calls, "semi-dodgy area."

"Mr. Rogers never visited this neighborhood. And, I really don't think I want any of them to be my neighbor."

She spots a late night movie theater. A horror film is being advertised on the marquee. The eyes of the aspiring writer light up. She has heard excellent reviews and is in dire need of an escape totally opposite of her present situation. Reality.

A parking space is effortlessly achieved.

"San Francisco, nah, nah, nah, nah, nah. And there's no meter either, demonic meter maid reader, hah!"

After paying for the ticket, she easily eases into a prime middle seat in the center section. Twenty minutes pass and this brings the theater to an almost full capacity.

"Real horror fans watch this type of quality by themselves. They are the true connoisseur of the macabre. And, Howard Phillips Lovecraft rests solidly on their bookshelf. These others, these cutesy couples and uneven quintets are mere impostors wishing they could understand. The Lovecraft Circle would not be known to them. What a shame! (you are) The Sham-sters.

"When at its artistic best, horror is like a fine wine or nicely aged brandy. Imagine five people simultaneously sipping a delicate wine from the same glass—talk about ridiculous tasting trough. Ick or rather ugh. That scenario is analogous to what's here in this cinema theater now.

"Horror in the vein of Howard Phillips L. is a symbiotic experience: You sit. It's there. You engage. It entertains (while inspiring somewhere within the undercurrent of your subconscious). You end. It's done. With the subtle simultaneous action one gets double the pleasure without much effort (or any at all) initiated by the intended to be entertained. That is one of the main beauties of the "Supernatural in Horror" as believed by me (coyly kissed with science and gently touched by teleology).

"However, as an undoubted Dot to a certified non-Dot, am I entertaining mere puerile fantasies that you, H.P. might just comprehend or prefer my presence? Even though I've looked beyond the limitations of your time pertaining to racialization—how can I rationally justify the admiration harboring in my mind regarding your prose, ponderings, and abundantly, overflowing talent? Maybe

Vladimir Soloviev or Mr. Upton Sinclair can assist with bringing luminescent clarity to this?"

After the film, she decides to explore her soon to be neighborhood via her automobile while erratic recent images from the motion picture move through her mind.

"Glad I saw. In the vein of Lovecraft, that wizard of word weavers, I welcome this glorious *"nebulous pageantry."*

She misses a few turns. The scenery and territory grow unfamiliar. Confusion mounts as her mental memory attempts to reorganize.

"Whomever designed this section of the city layout was not sober. That individual was drunk and chintzy was his choice.

Lovecraft's prose seeps into her mind. Verbatim.

"The most merciful thing in this world, I think, is the inability of the human mind to correlate all its contents. We live on a placid island of ignorance in the midst of black seas of infinity, and it was not meant that we should voyage far." (6)

She navigates her vehicle toward Sawtelle Boulevard for a midnight green tea, boba drink.

"Matcha. Gotcha. Cha, cha, cha."

While there, sitting in a chair, sipping brown boba through a straw, the young Bored One sees a man jump out of his SUV and shoots a pedestrian in a business suit with an orange, oversized super soaker. He has on run-of-the-mill blue jeans paired with a faded purple tie-dye tee shirt adorned with Jimi Hendrix. This 70s image catches the eye of the writer-to-be.

"Jimi the Hendrix. Sure'd be nice to touch that purple haze, Lysergic Acid Diethylamide be damned, John C. Lilly, M.D. But oh, when it comes to the scientists it's always, but always about Jack Whiteside Parsons and most definitely Tesla the infinitely beautiful wisdom of Nikola."

The Tie-dyed fires upon two more random people. Def Leppard's *Foolin'* is blazing from his vehicle, blaring into the night. Water freely flows forward into the open.

"Jeez. A truly bona fide refugee from responsibility. Oh yeah. Maybe just plain crazy—old-fashioned style. Or, the most popular option: LSD-25. Wanna 'nother hit, Jackson? Chased any pink elephants, yet? One hears of these things not witness. Ever."

Returning to the vehicle, she sits in the parking lot wrestling with her conscience.

"Goodness. What if that super soaker possessing individual just had a thorough and complete nervous breakdown? Think I'm not far behind in the losin' my mind department."

There is a worldwide popular diner chain down the street. Prices are cheap. It is not far from her storage either. The aspiring writer's shoulders slump forward while her lips take on a downward position. She is concerned. Deeply.

"I'm even caught up in that carousel of conundrums. Jeez, I'd better watch it. Paranoia, man. Besides, all throughout college no one ever refused to serve me or was super slow with coffee or pancakes."

An addendum thought fastly trails behind.

"Can you help me? (Fellow American). Enjoy life, man. Dun..dun..dun..dun.. dun..dun…Black Sabbath-n-Led Zeppelin—the 70s again. But more importantly, what the hell happened to real Rock-n-Roll? Heavy Metal time. Those guys and bands like 'em were profoundly producing sheer Portal Opening Music. Those lucky bum concert goers. I bet a few slipped through to the elsewheres in the space time continuum. AC/DC, I salute you."

She drives to the diner, gets out the car then opens the rear door in order to retrieve some reading material. A book falls out. It is by the author Bruce Rux. (7) (7a)

"Bruce Rux rocks! Bring it on home, tomodachi Rux. You are a demigod."

Gingerly, her hands pick up the book. Her eyes look off and upward to graciously gaze at the full moon.

"That man in Colorado Springs is indulging in some serious, serious mental manifestations. I know he has a circle of folks where the discussion delves deeply into the wildly intelligent. Wow! He's hot."

She clutches the book firmly to her chest.

"California. Colorado. Never been to the Rocky Mountain state or the Overlook Hotel for that matter. The secret fan from a not so far off land. Smile. The wild web of info. that man generates. Whew! I can never meet him though. It would taint and certainly tarnish the "image.""

Her beaming smile is not one induced out of joy but relief.

"I'm just waiting for the asteroid to hit, really. We need to begin again—start afresh, begin anew. Everything concerning this world is so incredibly askew." Eyeing the picturesque cover, her next comments are cued.

"Sci-Fi ain't ever hurt anybody. What scares me is a million man plus army possessing the full realization they will never marry and perhaps not have sex with a woman unless she is a relative. E-fuckin'-gad that's bad. That testosterone action needs no ninja hand signals to energize it's earth elements or chakra. Hmm…the explosion will be tremendously explosive. Speaking of things teetering then tumbling into the terrible…Depart from the East and concentrate on the colossal mess now rattling the West.

"Politics should remain where they belong: In the toilet. The cesspool of all that needs to be discarded, disposed, destroyed. That's where the political arena exists today. No Thinkers or Sophisticates. Just brutal greedy brutes obsessed with feeding an insatiable greed (an unconquerable need) to dominate. Send in the bankers! Fiat international insolence perpetuated by the ultimate knavish stratagem. Fear is their weapon—the infamous *them*—while simultaneously exercising as a convenient, comforting elixir to Citizen Ordinary. How scary. 'Look the other way as I delicately rape your soul, Prole.' Blind to things that create true happiness. Deaf to those whose words could possibly pacify the pain. Who's to be next in line in order to be tyrannically traumatized in a clandestine vein? An exercise extremely opposite of persistent compassion.

"No true diplomats anymore. Statesmen are extinct. Only politicians slink amongst us. The difference is solidified in the hardcore experience of a blasphemously abysmal reality felt more in the developing world than it is in the world of those who are in control. Farewell, David Lloyd George. Adieu, Monsieur Clemenceau. Your kind are welcome no more. For the preeminent festival of debauchery has just commenced.

"Why, the Marquis de Sade would surely want to shake the perpetrators' hands along with applying a proper peck on both cheeks. And you should be made aware the short sneaky wizard (accompanied by a newfangled, eldritch Tin Man and Dot) from the fabled land of Oz is to be in full attendance. That tricky Trickster has currently, fiercely pulled back the curtain exposing all to his conniving conveyances now ruthlessly reverberating throughout many lands.

"Hence, who really cares? Malevolent Takers have hijacked the conscience and will of the Doers and Carers. Apathy leads to abolition, obliteration. Ask any Carib that. More verbatim H.P., please. *"I ought to be hardened by this stage; but there are some experiences and intimations which scar too deeply to permit of healing, and leave only such an added sensitiveness that memory reinspires all the original horror."* (8) Some injustices remain forever untouched by the healing passage of time. The blatant chaining of pinyon trees in the '70s acutely comes to mind. (9) Their peril is eternal, undying, everlasting. May we all learn from the burns as we suffer the consequences.

"I wish I could see real ninjas fighting. Hmph, I strongly desire to call some now to straighten this screwy world out. Blazing chakra on fire—singe you! Boom! Hey, Cosmic Masters where the hell is that seriously overdue asteroid?! The super stellar blitz. For most of us are already the walking dead. We are counted as existing NOT experiencing life. Living is a figment and fragment dream sequence most refuse to acknowledge and certainly can't define.

"In the interim, everyone should fathom the fact that Captain Kathryn Janeway and the super clever crew of the U.S.S. Starship Voyager should be running this show. Uncharted territory conquered by strict, adhesive accordance to rockin' regulations—with science of the super natural kind to keep it all in line."

The young woman, along with her melancholy mood, slides into a cozy booth intended for four but is to be occupied currently, by a party of one. The semi-slanted eyes patiently peruse her immediate surroundings, while her mind methodically meanders.

"Sure there's a lot of ugly here. Untarnished impoverished existence spiritual and physical—vast urban decay. However, there's a lot more beauty aesthetically speaking and poetically feeling. Among the adjective-subjects to top my list is OPPORTUNITY. It's the most indicative of freedom. The ability to raise well above your categorized station and class level no matter what race, gender, religious preference or creed.

"America is like life. It's what you make of it. She's a young country. Give her time to mature into the realization that we are all man, human, mankind on one planet. Empire. Skim-pire.

"True empires went out and conquered, enslaved, installed a foreign god belief, gloriously exploited, initiated native language eradication, pillaged, overstretched then fell. And, we're talking continents not a country or two. Project U.S.A. splintered off from the Big Grand Dame of jolly ol' colonizers. Founded mainly by upper class businessmen (with wealthy landowning farmers being well accounted for) and has been run like a budding, burgeoning business enterprise ever since.

"Only problem, the CEOs of this experiment are rather illicitly covetous. Especially as of late. While midlevel managers and all below are benevolently benighted. Hence, the "fall" will simply be analogous to a 'Send Fail' in the vein of fax machine terms. Implosion. For the influence of the American Brand: soda pop, doll and coffee, darlin' will unyieldingly keep on being purchased. Suicide from within will definitely do US in. Trust me. Or rather, trust in the Lord. Right, McCready? Hmm…ponder ponder.

"It's the politicians, stupid (and remember there are no more diplomats) and those of us who intrinsically place them in power who should go. Not this *what could be so beautiful and enriching experience* of a nation. Alas, we are mired in wantonly fictitious hegemony with alarming alacrity. Ignorant people who cast ballots while on auto-pilot…Hmm…Let's see. Josef Stalin coined it well, "More like a "caveman Marxist." His curt, blunt descript of Chairman Mao applies to us, the Americans now. Less marxism, more caveman.

"Wait. Caveman Fascist. For only a super killing fiend finely figures out the mind and intentions of his counterpart. Leader you are not. Some folks should remain locked up in the back room, possibly chained to the bed—1930s style. Or, at the very least, securely sequestered to the sideline of 21st Century life.

"Crazy cousin Johnny and his spiritual gangsters (along with their band of inelegant, imbecilic and thoroughly inane cohorts) should not sit in seats of power—contentedly in control of a massive superpowerful military armed with supertech killing machines. The only thing which need remain in their possession, reminiscent of any power, are a patrol of aging G.I. Joe dolls along with their tiny black plastic machine guns instead of the real deal."

The maddening, inner mental gestations of the aspiring writer rages onward.

"Your patriotic smoke screen does not fool US all. Some are dismally coherent as this nation is dragged to a most momentous fall. The tremendous temptation to reminisce of days absent of blatant fear and a gripping, stupefying ignorance running concurrently with the acute destruction of democracy…Your engagement in a decadent parody of plain speak while a smattering of citizens recognize your feeble, yet furtive and unceasing endeavor to render our Rights from the Bill and Constitution into mere, paltry palimpsests…

"Good God! But you make the very essence of my psyche wretchedly recoil. Such disrespect done to George Mason and all other (frank) Founding Fathers…Hmm…to quote the great Lovecraft once more (semi-verbatim), it's "…altogether too wild to believe. Such things "do" not happen in any normal world." (10)

"Tinkering with time with failed, futile attempts to adjust our fate (and others not within these borders)…transcending boundaries not meant for any decent, sane man to tread. Hello, Alaska! Time to drill, ravage, spoil. The land belongs to no one. Only mother nature (and a few publicity-shy tree spirits) are justifiable stewards. Oh Chief Joseph if we ever needed you, it's now. And how! We are all too infantile to deserve your benevolence, Ms. Big Blue Marble. I implore you as you heed this contemplation, send in the asteroid, please God, Cosmic Masters,

Budda or YWH. Or, whomever is the current Guardian on duty shift for the Milky Way.

The Cosmos and beyond are destined for the divine ones to dwell so, when the mangy protagonists (the individuals) concerned are extreme cases of non-nimble-wits? How dreadfully, dastardly appalling!

"There is no such thing as *premonitious* defense. And as for your self-promoting offense mantra: the hand that can't be cut off, must be kissed? My compassion is crippled by the inaction of us all. A sure cure rests in new tech and less fossil fuel addiction. To accurately address this garish distress, some words will never, ever aptly apply. *With this stuff, you smell it and "they" do the laughing.* No matter what dialect. No matter what language. Subconscious born, homegrown adages do come close. Oh my.

"Alas, as for the bankers—a neoteric, acutely customized board game of Monopoly will do. No more twisted real-life games of World Screw for you and your band of feckless goon crew.

"Not even the great Western society's Almighty God can rectify this wholly deplorable situation now definitely deleterious to us all. A divine team is required. Talk about Team Spirit."

Pausing, and looking off a calming, temporary resolution is allowed to resurface from her subconscious and lull the negative vivifications currently percolating her cerebral complement.

"A solid, un-surreal Plan B (forgoing the "Voyager-Janeway" solution) which could most definitely stave off the miasma of maniacal mania at present, is to deploy the dependable, determined diligence of the omnipotent librarians. A lone agent of your field shall do nicely.

"All hail to those un-harrowing harbingers of blissful neutrality and the almighty written word. Knowledge and intellect is abundantly exposed and spontaneously deployed amidst your perseity. And, a female, in an eminent position is a most balancing element when being bodacious with poise, grace and grandeur.

"Your ilk once saved me from diabolical gym teachers of both my junior and high school years with notes depicting an insistent need for my presence amongst the books as opposed to in the punishing fields and on the unforgiving blacktops with the p.e. professors. Now, I can rest assured, one will save us all from total deterioration."

The sharp, hurried words of an order being barked to a tired waitress cuts into her concentration. When the semi-slanted eyes of the aspiring writer land on the speaker, her mind takes a detour from historical figures to current, modern physiques.

"Obesity seems to be making a big comeback. No pun intended—honey bun. I wonder if the secret government—the real mofos running this raggedy masquerade passing as modern civilization—is fattening them up for a Lloyd Bochner star turn, 'Hello my space brothers. How are we to be served?'

"It's not so much the extra poundage. That, can be resolved through surgical intervention or extreme determination which includes weights (and perhaps a diligent fast and cleanse). But at 3:45 a.m. don't these people have nightmares? Chili cheese fries, double cheeseburger, thick milkshake and apple pie dessert: After this grandiose consumption of superfatty, heavy, nutrition-free foods where is one's mind? Their blood is in their stomach helping to digest but, the brain, the mind, the psyche—what is it doing while all that blood (and precious H_2O) is being diverted from other organs then swiftly supplied to the below? *Meat's meat and man's gotta eat!* Just ask Farmer Vincent.

"I have enough inner battle turmoil with my quasi-vegetarian diet. And, my dreams are becoming more vividly violent. Perhaps it's just me? Like the death mobile being effected by the wind on the 5 that time. I wonder if I'm going insane?"

The hidden ceiling speakers spew forth a weak strain of *I think I'm goin' outta my head* (muzak version).

"Seems like they're playing my tune. I never realized how many versions existed and the variety of people who did this song. More importantly, it never seemed so prevalent before tonight. Perhaps it's a sign? A bitter tainted omen of my near future? A most pertinent quote surfaces, 'We are at the mercy of our biochemistry, one error at the molecular level can wreck our lives and turn us into lunatics.' (11) Damn you de Ropp! And, damn myself for reading him.

Better still I could just be paranoid. Paranoia is a phobia though. I believe phobic possessing people are not uncommon in the nut house—the dreaded insane asylum. To be institutionalized. That's not the place to be.

"I wonder how they do it these days? Do people with white jackets just appear in your immediate vicinity—providing a window of lucidity with words spoken in soft, soothing tones, "Get into the vehicle. Let's take a peaceful ride to serenity." Or, after Reagan closed down the state mental institutions, while he was governor of this state, is it possible the aforementioned image portrayed can now only be found in movies, old books, and disjointed faded memories buried within the shredded awareness of some of the older homeless people who are securely locked in bona fide insanity? Hmm…not a topic I wish to ponder ponder.

"There's always this vague fear of psychosomaticism kicking in and sneaking through the back door of your consciousness then firing up the propensity to nut up. Jeez."

The shrill voice of a diner seated two tables away grabs her attention. She appears to be a little tipsy and is cussing out the waiter for a small infraction on his part.

"Wishing he was finished with that woman…She reminds me of a person who goes on a 5 day 4 night vacation to some island, gets sloppy drunk…says the wrong thing at the right time to another drunk vacationer, gets beat down then screws a black native guy in the water somewhere in order to redeem it all—whatever the fuck that means. Hmm…ponder."

Her inquisitive semi-slanted eyes follow the same waiter as he goes to his next patrons. Both are on the pudgy, dowdy side. Female.

"What an almost prostituting quality this scene has. The tired waiter, maybe model, maybe student—definitely not an actor (aspiring or otherwise)."

The two chunky female patrons blatantly eye him and toss flirtatious words his way.

"Makin' big jokes but, I'm only doing the ho hum, while they are grinnin' and giggling. He's deflecting those mots like a midlevel ninja. Baby, call up the perpetual wind tunnel deflection skill. Nothing can penetrate that—at least not what they've got. That twosome's fantasy fuckin' him while he wants a reality tip (nice size, please). Maybe he has a girlfriend? Perhaps she's super young, fit, incredibly attractive and most likely sleeping around on him. Sometimes she uses a condom. Most of the time not.

"Who's the daddy? Where's her daddy? Who's your Daddy? God but I despise that saying. Now, it's kickin' around in my mind."

The aspiring writer's attention leaves the trio.

"Hey, it's the 21st Century. He could openly have a boyfriend. Wow, why stop there…"

The aspiring writer unsuccessfully stifles a chuckle as the next image enters her mind. She whispers aloud,

"Animal lover." Her eyes widen. "Where'd that come from? Whoa. What's the difference between super duper tired (a la being extremely fatigued) and being drunk? Insanity. The former, I firmly believe withholds a twisty yet tangible path leading semi-directly to the nut house. Straight jacket, padded room. No visitors. Never. Especially if you're a Dot. Oh, wait. Then you could become "useful to society." Experiment time. Send in the scientists! Last name preferred? Cameron, M.D. One's mind can only withstand so much.

"At least with liquor one is merely suffocating thus killing off brain cells. (12) So, fewer remain to nut up with. Should I order some rum with my coffee? Wish I could but, it's too late. Hmm…ponder ponder."

A couple engaged in heavily performed P.D.A. in a nearby booth next are the focal point of her observation.

"Soul mate? Mine? True happiness? There's something I cannot feel. Hah. Looking for someone (Him) to show me things that I can't find. He's dead. Expired before lighting my fire. This is a violent ass world. Grotesque, unkind times. Grisly days paired with tumultuous nights. Damn, and I never got a chance to see what he looked like. And, where's that asteroid? Goodness.

"Or better still, what about Dick van Patten holding a needle, or was it a mask hooked up to noxious, toxic gas? (13) Where is he? Where is that poised, pleasant grin? The building housing the rooms where lovely scenery depicting unspoiled wilderness cordially bestowed before your visual field, as your eyes close for a final time should do the jump from the celluloid in order to be the other choice as opposed to the dastardly deferred asteroid.

"Democracy holds no place in the spirit world. For surely the majority of the majority of the souls inhabiting this planet, in this physical reality, desire to move the hell on. Evolve! Resolve! No longer to dissolve in misery and immense uncertainty concerning their overall well being. Hmm…must not be depressed."

She views her book.

"My eyes are tired. And, this coffee is getting cold. Things, my energy mainly, is winding down. Funny the sky is beginning to illuminate."

A crooked smile crosses the aspiring writer's face.

"Funnier still if it is that asteroid. I have only one word. Finally. One must ponder no more."

Absently, her hands fluff out her short, black curly hair. The semi-slanted eyes give an extended blink, a subtle smile conquers the crooked smirk while simultaneously playing at both corners of the bow shaped mouth. Lucidity is returning to the aspiring writer as she exits the diner, and slides into her automobile.

"Moving—domicile style—cures most mental manias. Nothing like continuous hard work. Labor intense, David Bowie "Let's Dance," video style. Pulling, tugging, lifting. Oh glory." (14)

The early morning light from the sun abundantly adds to her clarity as she pulls into the parking lot of the storage center. Instigated by the light of the sun, the aspect of another soul mate being realized brightens the arena of her awakening aura.

"The night before fades to no more as daybreak provides no escape. Perhaps if I now aspire to obtain a male partner, my desire should be elevated to pursue one who is in fact me, only simultaneously subsisting on a higher vibrational frequency—that is the genuine meaning of helping oneself."

She effortlessly angles the auto into a stall then opens the door.

"Narcissistic reverie aside, I am seriously contemplating initiating the process (perhaps) of putting forth a righteous request for a refund pertaining to this prolonged, packaged tour of the third dimension. However, as the Science (Fiction) master craftsman (Arthur C. Clarke) stated through Nicole des Jardins Wakefield, *'Timor Mortis conturbat me.'* I'm in enthusiastic accordance with this fragment from a long ago Latin poem."

After 2 years and 2 months of her belongings being in storage (while traipsing in the Orient), this aspiring writer's gotta move to do.

"All night long I've thought of things. I've told you now of my state (of being). Writer-to-be, that's me. Now, we've reached the end."

"The subconscious does not actually like to be called the subconscious at all; it is really our first consciousness, a combination of physical and emotional consciousness."

Genevieve Paulson, *Kundalini and the Chakras*

Sorta 32 questions on a cold winter's day

◆

*shen brevard
Tokyo winter 2003*

How bad is second hand smoke? Sure, it smells terrible or at the most is vastly different from fresh air. However, airborne carcinogens are found more and more in abundance in today's polluted society. The all burning inquiry that I'm mentally mired in momentarily is: What is love? Is it based on harmonics? And if so, does lust fall into this flux somewhere in between? Why is the mind consistently fuzzy both during a budding romance and a devastating heartbreak? What can counter this overpowering effect? Self-control? Is true, genuine celibacy and abstinence from all forms of sexual affection undoubtedly possible? Once achieved, can an individual attain a resounding satisfaction in life? I must see, wish/desire to discover if self-love and self-containment are possible however, forever loosely connected to this ponderance is the age old question which for an answer would be great: Why don't men call? Even the ones who are interested? How long must one wait until attaining this information or…Profiles.

Why are some people devastatingly gorgeous from certain angles while overtly mediocre from a different perspective? Same individual, same observer. Different conclusion entirely. A wailing child attracts my attention. Other toddlers are waddling away from the screamer. A calm, cluster of mothers observe motionlessly nearby. I wonder if the howling tot will pass her 'Park Debut?' Wonder if this is a trial run or the deed is being done and sealed? My inner thoughts beckon once more.

Does a craft choose a person or does an artisan perfect a desire to create? Why is it that the silence of a solitary existence is cherished some of the time yet, viewed as ironclad proof of rejection by societal peers in other moments?

Sick-n-Single
(the breakdown)

◆

shen brevard
Los Angeles (Beverlywood Bungalow) fall
2004

Sunday, the eternal fun day

Sunday, for as long as I can remember, has always been my favorite day of the week. My parents were not the religious type so, it has nothing to do with church, God or the popular "Christian" day of rest. I must add they were not anticlerical either. The parental unit that is. Looking back on my churchless youth days (which were wholeheartedly filled with deep reverence of a divine spirit, mind you), two quotes from one Professor F. G. Gregory in the vein of Dostoyevsky suits just nicely.

"When fools start listening to atheists society shudders…" "The concept of God is socially valuable if only to keep the *Smerdiakovs* in order." (15)

Oh yes, religion was respected while not being force fed in any hellbent manner whatsoever.

"Cough, cough."

There were neither Buddhist chants nor Hindu mantras hovering within my vicinity either. Thought I might include this as it is quite pertinent since I am a native of the West Coast of the young U.S.A.

"Cough, cough."

Excuse me. Y'see, since the wee hours of the morning, I have been lousily fighting a losing battle against a rather stubborn sniffle and doggedly scratchy throat. Both of which are gaining ground rapidly thus escalating into a deep rattling cough coupled with a burning, raw sinus passage. I'll try not to get too descriptive but, I do foresee my current health condition perhaps indirectly (if not directly) contributing to an otherwise neutral narrative tone. An advanced apology is in order. Please do accept.

Back to the fun of the Sunday. The six days of the week preceding it, can be rather sensationally daunting for some—present company included.

Grateful not to be included in the burgeoning unemployment stats—so freely and eagerly—displayed on the evening news shows and splashed across random internet web sites…

But is being trapped in a binding, lackluster cog style duty a fulfillment or testament to one's ultimate destiny? Food-n-lodging aside, do you really need gadgets? Are modern do-dads going to assist in self-evolvement? Truth be told, they are sold in order for you to subsist in this binding, grinding hold.

There are things that adults do and children aren't supposed to see. Per chance, the deal twists and to everyone's bemusement (and slight confusement) the kids perceive then perfect this confounding gist.

The foolish may frown yet not so long ago when the fourth month was marked as the first of the year, responsible society was in control. In stepped the smart, authoritative adepts and January took the place of April leaving the "true" first for only pundits to remember and fools to accept. The French made sure the rest of the West was never to forget the then great, tragic brainwash since they are just the ever so 'hep hip.'

Who were these 'month swamping' rabble rousers? Why, the ancestors of today's 'spiritual gangsters.'

They've been formidably forewarned by the Persians though, "May God kill him who himself does not know but presumes to guide others to the doors of his kingdom."

For this is truly the age of the lame man! And, I am not talkin' 'bout an adjective pertaining to a walking stance. Hint, clue, big style—right in front of you: more like in the vein of Nietzsche's "last man."

But, more of the fluff stuff reason as to why Sunday is the one day which just "does it" for me. Television from my youth to adolescence. Examples requested? Case history provided. Just plain, fun craggily news journalists sarcastically and entertainingly exposing (while introducing a plethora of 'reaching for the dictionary' verbiage) an' up til then bad ass crooked human, whose woeful deeds of deceit were shrouded oh so secretly. I can see the clammy perspiration fastly forming upon their foreheads. The surprised looks of horror and doors rapidly slamming in the cameras as they kept rolling. Caught. Busted. And, the news was still trusted. A trial was held then shortly that same somebody was justly jailed. Or, fleein' across the sea no longer to return give or take two to twenty-five years. Oh gee.

Then there was the venerable Jessica Fletcher cycling the pathways of Cabot Cove, Maine, typing away on an old fashioned black colored typewriter and solving mysteries-n-murder both in the domestic and international locale. McGarrett, Dano and Chin of the exotic Sandwich Islands, later to be more popularly known as The Hawai'ian Islands. The show was none other than the hip hula movin' themed *Hawai'i Five-O*. At one point that was a big Sunday event-er.

It was passed on to me during my travels, by some illustrious all knowing trivia induced individual in regards to Jack Lord auditioning for the role of the space faring Captain James Tiberius Kirk. Jeez, imagine Dano as Scotty (or as Chekov?) and who would have been Spock and Bones? More to the point, how true is this information? The validity could be tainted. But, when one begins to put forth the effort to investigate such nonsensical nonsense, they have already lost control of essential living. Time is precious. Every moment counts. Better to just keep wondering or perpetuating a most ingenuous, albeit innocuous, t.v. trivia falsehood than give in to dedicating precious life experiencing time due to the whimsical words of a fellow generation X-er.

"Cough. Cough."

Barnaby Jones slides into the memory lane excursion (with the cool theme music) as does *The Man from Atlantis* (if memory serves me correctly). The last three though, not sure their original air date was the blessed Sunday but, I'm sure syndication found them making an appearance at least once. And another white haired man, though a well established ecologist and naturalist long before gracing his presence in front of the camera, Marlin Perkins of *Wild Kingdom* fame. To this very day I hope to embark upon a most engaging African safari.

Ah, Sunday, the forever knowledge bestowing day.

Elimination through Illumination

Speaking of granting knowledge—a friendly neighborhood neo-Hippie recently warned me (as I was taking my coffee house destination stroll) against the many insidious dangers and thoroughly damaging side effects effected upon one's being by the dreaded fluorescent light. These thoughts and other odd little factoids reminiscent to them never seem to come to the forefront of one's conscience until third dimensional awareness is down and mania takes advantage of an ample opportunity to cross the threshold. I call it…

"Cough, cough, sniff, blow, blow."

…the 'Creep-in.'

Don't step on a crack in the sidewalk.

Don't talk with food in your mouth.

Don't smack that same nourishment, either.

Don't masturbate (but it's extremely beneficial to thoroughly masticate).

Don't stare (even though most modern society dwellers do—a little too much in my opinion (especially on the freeway) but, who's asking?).

Do not let a pole separate you and an amicable walking companion.

"Bluh."

Watch out for the infamous 'black cat' (But, what if one is owned by you?) Hmm…

My throat. Jeez I need to get out of this room. Things are becoming a bit confining and slightly…

"Blow, blow, ha-chuu."

…confounding. Once the Creep-in's initial stage has been achieved, Phase II is effortlessly ushered into reality. And, at this interval or level, a most ambitiously built apparatus is brought into the picture. Fluorescent lights will eliminate a lot of people (along with destroying their astral selves). The event shall be played out like *Logan's Run* when a person reached the age of 30. The big bye-bye. The see ya no more sayoonara. Hmm…why some enterprising soul will come up with a t.v. show.

I can see it now, *Closet Charlie*. In regards to his duty in life's preference he's just 'come out' so to speak as the new office supply guy for the company. He doubles as the man-fiend ushering all fluorescent light afflicted into another place (where no animate objects twitch or stir). So, while some may believe his 'coming out' of the closet refers to a certain sexual preference, the actual fact deals with his accepting his fate as a demonic office supply guy. He's coming out while you're going in (to oblivion)!

"Hey, has anyone seen Stacy? She's been gone a while." "No, no, come to think of it, I haven't. Last time I saw her, she was going to get some paper clips from the supply guy." Muha hah hah. Well, that's strange.

"Cough. Cough. Cough. Snort. Blow. Blow."

Okay, here I go. Must prepare to penetrate the outside world flow. Sitting up is the first step to getting up thus getting in-n-out and the whole process over! I can see me now, in the parking lot after the task is complete.

Everyone's tryin' to 'make it.' And, I would have made it. I will do a victory dance coupled with a 'hooray-for-applesauce' chant if I make it out of the store with all my astral selves in tact.

"Cough, rattle, heh chu!"

Oh man but I despise having to mingle with even a small fraction of the mass especially with stamina at half mast. And that was just the mapped out mental plan. Wait until the for real reality deal. Hmm…

It's gonna take what I coin the "Wonder Twin-less" action. No twin possessin'' am I however; must summon enough insta-energy into existence (albeit the surplus lasting no longer than an extended 11 minutes) to complete untold tasks and successfully achieve seemingly impossible cerebral and select physical feats. Konnichiwa, Cat Jaguar!

Hellmute be damned

And that brings to mind the, *when and why did that happen* mergence (or attainment) of a certain British car maker by an American brand. The roadways hold some unpredictable curves. Thank goodness my mind and mental affairs aren't caught up in that twisted land. Commuting though, has me firmly by the hand.

There are rules to follow and life preserving action to abide by while commuting in a modern megalopolis.

Although I try not to allow my eyes to stray much farther than my immediate two vehicles ahead of me-vicinity. One never knows what sights or kinda action one can get into the next vehicle over. But where oh where must one's vision take them? After sixty minutes the attention goes astrayin'.

Traffic, smaffic, I just can't crack it! For surely something this dastardly dwelling is not of this beautiful Earth? If thought of as originating from Hell itself, or, uh, manmade induced calamities, well, then it's almost palpable. But, then again, to some the entire concept of Hell's existence is but for the frivolously foolish and delightfully dimwitted. They—the brilliant geniuses—need to be on the Yamanote-sen or Okadkyu-line of good ol' Edo-town. Or, better still, the Interstate 405 South which sometimes goes by the graciously deceiving moniker, 'San Diego Freeway.' Have them, the super intellect sophisticate sect, placidly placed amidst this human chaos of stagnation. Hmm…wonder how the benevolently bourgeois brood would categorize that stagnating stifle of human interlude? Anyone for a Quaalude?

"Cough, gasp, ah."

The hellmute is what it is. There. Ugly. A surreal test of both one's patience and challenge to their adherence to solid moral infused upbringing if one even, ever existed. The older I get—or is it the more social situations I encounter?—seems to present me with a picture where most modern day individuals do not possess common courtesy within their vocabulary. Feral. Nefarious. Unschooled. These are concept-adjectives practiced with wild abandonment. That's a definite 'For Sure-er.' The uncannily uncouth. It's their time to shine. While those in the minority just bitch…"cough, sniff."..moan…"heychu!"…and whine.

"Sniiiiiiffff. Ugh."

Hmm…better throw on the proverbial sweats and make a run for the store. Hah! But, let's not kid ourselves. I'm in no condition for a jog or even a brisk walk. Why it pains me just to stand and breathe—simultaneously. How the hell am I to survive, getting dressed, brushing my teeth, throwing a cap on the disheveled hairdo, maneuvering a motor vehicle (even though just a few blocks away), picking up 'over the counter' meds, trying to stay focused on perceived reality while all lucidity is rapidly unraveling, most likely stand in an endless line (yes the 8 items or less queue tends to warp known time in circumstances such as these), then returning home to the comfort and semi-coziness of my residence? Who knows? Who cares? Guess I should. But, my apprehension is beyond concern, it's worry and more to the point: Fear.

A stark raving fright that accidents can happen, embarrassment is high on the list when engaging in interactive activities while in the throes of the initial stages of a good old fashioned hearty cold. Bluh!

"Cough, sniff, sniff, cough, rattle."

The most contagious contagion (Is that redundant? And if so, does it make grammatically correct sense? Ah, the Creep-in! Or rather, shades of it.) is the good ol' human yawn. Pause right here to contemplate this statement. Quite effective stop. The Yawn.

A most innocent enigma. It's ploy so benign. One doesn't even have to see it, merely hear its call then heed its command upon their being. Alas, there is no helping hand. Alone I live, with no one am I involved so, lone I shall tread to the "store." Must put forth a most ambitious effort to quiet this mind as well. Soon-ish.

Quickly dress, don a cap and out into the cold I step. A light drizzle meets me. The roar of a passing city bus suddenly assaults my audio senses in order to greet me.

There is a stark similarity in regards to the controlled wildness of the unpredictable deftly displayed driving antics put on by both San Francisco MUNI operators and Santa Monica Big Blue Bus drivers. Not as familiar with Big Blue but have seen it slickin' around the streets of the Southland long enough to realize, recognize, when pressed those operators are cut from the same foraying cloth as their MUNI compatriots up North.

The Blue and the Orange

I enter the dry safe haven of my vehicle.

The Blue-n-the Orange versus the individual motor vehicle and sometimes stray pedestrian or even a stubborn cyclist. How critical.

Let me relax behind my steering wheel here just for a moment.

Fond memories of MUNI days seep into my mind.

First mental picture manifestation: the infamous gate leading to San Francisco's Chinatown. Tourists, noisome crowds and narrow little streets aside, the image which looms large is the 30 Stockton electric bus.

My best friend in high school's father was an actual employee of MUNI. When pulled from the office and forced into the field, oh, the stories of gore and glory would he ever yield. My fondest involved the 30 Stockton.

It's route crossed various neighborhoods of the famed City by the Bay. The stretch coursing through Chinatown proved to be the most adventurous jaunt. Sometimes people, after paying a pilgrimage to the fish market, would board along with other bus catching folks. These people with their "fresh" catches sometimes loosely held plastic bags filled with water transporting live specimen (soon to be meal deal).

One day, an older woman with her 'omninous' plastic bag boarded the 30 with my best bud's Dad behind the wheel. Needless to say, it did not take long for the bus to come to a most jerking stop (the poles continuously seemed to fall on those particular coaches) and the bag was let loose spilling the water and three small, still live and very active squid onto the floor of the 30 Stockton. It was midday during a downtime for tourist season so, the shock value was kept to a minimum. However, even some of the seasoned locals were not prepared to dodge that woman's would-be dinner as it slid and oozed up and down the aisle. Wow. Now, that's some bus catchin' for ya!

An actual interactive MUNI episode I participated in (or at least was present) concerned a rather grouchy, slightly overweight bus driver. I heard somewhere plump people tend to be rather pleasant. Heard of Jolly ol' Saint Nick? Well, this man was nowhere in the neighborhood of nice. Case in point: When several passengers boarded with a rather large map in hand, he grimaced.

The tension in the air escalated even more when the de facto leader of the bunch attempted in broken English to inquire if the 41 Union would be able to take them to their desired destination. Well, two things at the moment happened that became a 'first' for me in my young teenage existence. One, the fact that these were indeed Caucasians yet, did not seem to grasp the ability to speak English (American style) and two, the prolific profanity spewing from the mouth of the rotund MUNI driver.

Looking back, they were probably from a Slavic nation or maybe even Germany, since I was unfamiliar with their accent. However, to actually witness someone being cussed out on the bus, yeah, now, that was a first. And, they were innocent tourists. How tripped out. Well, they didn't remain on Mr. nonJolly's coach for long at all. Talk about not being sheltered anymore!

I ease further back into the comfort of the driver's seat. The soft pelting of the rain upon the car is proving to be rather soothing.

Random snippets of my MUNI riding days continue to play before my tired mind.
Here are the certain lines which seemed to get their super duper kicks by passing up would have been passengers even when a few more could have safely climbed aboard. The 38 Geary was notorious for perpetrating this behaviour. (16) With the 29 Sunset being a solid second—especially when it was in the vicinity of both San Francisco City College and Balboa BART station.

And, wait, here are the drivers of the 28 19th Avenue stopping at a corner mini store to buy Lotto tickets, a little too faithfully. Just pass Lincoln High School and sorta near Golden Gate Park...

Must not forget leaving my car parked at SFSU for a night course and catching the bus. But, sometimes a guy in my night course, who I had a crush on and he on me, would drive me home. He was from Santa Rosa but, now lived in S.F. Ahem. And, the car would stay overnight. When that happened, I would then catch the 43 Marina, not sure how but, it was achieved, and...Oh yes! Just remembered.

"Cough. Sniff. Cough."

Would take the M Oceanview (an Light Rapid Vehicle known in the fabled past as a streetcar and back then they were green and yellow) to Forest Hills station. After passing through West Portal, the "M" would become an underground streetcar. Also joining in this transformation were the L Taraval (which above the ground route took it to the avenues then onto the Ocean Beach area) and the K Ingleside, a most strange path it wove. Since it was the shortest if I'm not mistaken. It did however, take one to Balboa BART station where an effortless transfer to the infamous Bay Area Rapid Transit (BART) train lead to even further far flung destinations for those without cars or without desire to drive their automobiles. The final two LRV lines were the J Church and N Judah. They made their underground transformation elsewhere. Back to the 43 though.

Forest Hills for the longest time was a dump of a station. Wires whose existence none of us innocent patrons knew what purpose served were freely dangling from above exposed. Forever dimmed yellowish lights which only provided a 'who's gonna be slashed next atmosphere.' And, the infernal eeking of rats. Never seen however their eerily echoing song was delivered with such force one was not remiss to guess their girth and width. All-in-all, the condition of Forest Hills Station was such as it was.

Like it existed when San Francisco was known as Yerba Buena. And, it hadn't been too long since the Spanish semi-snatched it from the Russian fur trappers (at least where Northern Cal is concerned). But, this is way off track and so far in the past. The 43 Marina would stop at Forest Hills Station, above the ground, of course. And, the elevator was as slow as a super slackin' straggler. As for hoofin' it out on the stairs, well, remember that rodent callin'? The stairwell was dark and confined so…Didn't make any sense whatsoever since this is a pretty upscale, well-to-do neighborhood.

So, they, the taxpayers (I suppose) spiffed it up sorta around the same time the quaint Stonestown outdoor Mall (complete with Red Chimney restaurant and Judy's clothing boutique) underwent a major makeover and became the Stonestown Galleria. All this of course conveniently occurred after I graduated from Lowell High so, not to be enjoyed by either me or my high schooling compadres. And so, back to the 43 Marina.

The 43 line—heading in the direction toward the gracious Golden Gate Bridge—would end at the San Francisco Marina near the Presidio Military Base. Yes, spectacular views were experienced by anyone who took the time to appreciate. The Golden Gate Bridge, the Bay itself and from the angle of Crissy Field, on a clear day with no fog, viewing the Farallone Islands. Who, for most of us, while growing up in San Francisco, innocently mistook them for the Hawai'ian Islands. Talk about beyond 20/20 vision! The ability to see five hours away (no tail wind assistance either). The bionic Bay Area Babes. Hmm…Oh, and, the infamous Safeway Marina (a grocery store) was nearby as well. It was known as an unofficial possible meeting place for those seeking single heterosexual men with class—at least back then, not sure about the now—I even took a spin with my cart a few times in that store.

"Hey chu!" Bless me or rather that.

But, the best thing about the 43 Marina, and its final destination, was it fell within 20 good walking strides to a section of the Presidio (Fort Mason) where the San Francisco Public Library from time to time (first or third Wednesday of every month) (17) hosted a book sale. The volumes of literary exploits one could find at that locale were phenomenal! And, this is grossly underrated as stated. I remember a time where it would get pretty intense though amongst those stacks. For y'see a few savvy, and I coin 'frugal' book buyers for bookstores would be perusing with us independent, average Joe and Josephina literary lovers. And, if one weren't alert, the dastardly book buyer with a seemingly endless bank account, would snatch a rare find right out of your unclenched hand! There goes that deal. The intentional steal.

And, for some bizarre reason, the radio station Coit 93 FM would always be wafting through the Book Depot and on my dial in my car at that time (when the tape player wasn't playing jazz that is). Such like minds. Ah. And, they played the song "Steal Away" quite frequently back then (and sometimes Manilow's "I Write the Songs"). Such themes conjure up visions of meandering scenic drives. Which leads to driving on the 92 South.

Many times I trod that piece of highway. But, the only time which vividly stands out is once. While heading towards Monterey to Bay Books (a bookstore) most likely wrestling with the ongoing battle of emotional depression and seeing a MUNI bus, not even chartered, cruising down the highway. No number. No passengers. No sign. If memory serves me correctly, I do not believe the driver was in full uniform. And, in that precious, particular instance in time, MUNI became its meaning in the Far East: Adept Guru—due to the serene facial expression of that man. Forever will it be up there with the ultimate where total carefreeness and existing in a state of 'just being cool with it all' is etched upon the list of the best of the best.

Back Alley Baby

Uh oh. Must go back inside. Forgot my wallet. Ugh.

"*Best.*" Hah. Here's a glum connector of the personal nature. Wait, though, must learn to first somehow cut down on the mental ramble rattle. Perhaps when I am in better health? Too much on my plate as of late. Henceforth the girl can keep on with the circuitous contemplate.

"Sniff. Sniff."

Where's that damn thing? Okay, there's money on my dresser but the wallet I prefer.

"Sneeze. Hey-chu."

So, I've made it from the bedroom and now stand amidst a mess of a kitchen. How can one woman who's severely *culinarily* challenged create such a multitudinous mess?!

Dishwashing at times, can be very therapeutic though. The super-adhesive 'pancake mix-like' substance that only a bristle pad can eradicate? Why it's highly reminiscent to the jerk in the office who won't go away and get out of your personal face space until you cough (death rattle style) or inform them you proudly voted for Leonard Peltier on election day. Sudsy, soapy glasses is the (foam) head of all the beer you just simply must cut back on before you sleep with the wrong person. But, alas, wine is my Dionysian vice where brain cell killin' choices align. So, I guess this observation does not apply to me all the way. Be aware though, note to myself, they say 'two buck Chuck' can be just as date appearance deluding. Wonder if the 'Fearless Flyer' mentions that fun factoid?

But when in the throes of a twistin' tummy ache and thoroughly sore, hell fire chest feeling, dish doin' just adds to the ruin of everything. Which brings me to ponder, why haven't paper pots and pans been invented? I mean yeah, any idiot realizes fire and paper usually aren't the most compatible when their molecules meet however; with all the SUPERtechnology possessed by Japan and the U.S. military that's not too much of a request.

"Ugh."

Oh, but it's for the best. Speaking of 'best' here's the terrible memory which serves as an excellent connector to several previous thoughts ago. Hmm...

"Blow. Blow. Sniff. Snort."

Not like he was practicing hardcore monogamy. Never can one forget...

"Cough, cough, ugh, oh."

...Excuse me. That slipped through and was most uncontrollable. But, back to dating and faithfulness (or lack thereof). My mind will always remember him in the tiny, slight arms of Mindy or Wendy or whatever the cheatee female's name was. I prefer Lulu Trixiebelle. Just adds to the cheapness, busted deceit and overall seediness of it all. No one's named that really—at least where serious, life changing events such as relationship meltdowns are concerned.

And if my memory is pealing the clarity bell, I was over there in order to wash his dirty dishes since he was ill. Hah. What a sordid shame it is when one's love life history strongly resembles a psychomimetic world. So much for surprise romance. But, hey, for something like that, even the location should be a bit sullied and surreal.

Why not an alley for a fitting location? Somewhere near the garment district in the bowels of downtown L.A.? Y'know? Near the Public Library, circa 6th street area. Can an area be circa? Or, is it just reserved exclusively for eras? Oh, but I guess it's just the 'Creep-in.'

People just don't ask these types of questions. It's just not put out there, y'know? And, for those who do dare to bring it up—who's gonna wanna engage them? That's when people create people. The ones who'll talk to you, all right. All the time. For your ears only. Invisible to all but the creator himself. Invisible friends who are fondly remembered as childhood created intellect while deadly dreaded as one matures. But, never ever knock the beauty of the brain dominated by the right side. One must always take heed of W. Compton Leith's "Sirenica" (1927), 'but woe to those who are made to dream the creator's dream without his finer understanding or his skill of capture.' (18)

Yes, there exists a fine line of dulling the chaotic while courtin' its skill.

Fat affect aphrodisiac. Transcendence over dependence : Savior through the literary salvation.

Must make mirror check before leaving again. Hmm...the reflection.

Start another day, gain another pound. The sweats are a bit tight-ish. Oh no. The thighs, okay easy melt away but, to have a semblance of a pantyline when none are adorned and that damned middle section transforming from a noticeable "barely there bulge" to a 'hey there to ya, salute!"…

Oh but sweet Jesus. The pounds are starting to get a little too comfortable around my middle area. Before long, if I don't keep up a rather watchful eye, an all out invasion of flab will ravenously descend upon my rather fragile physique.

Yeah, better start evicting the soft before it hardens and starts sending for "fat" assault teams.

Exercise, gym or a good brisk walk can chase, capture and eradicate most excess as long as the thyroid gland isn't orchestrating an obese band plan. It all boils down to greed, need and the lazy steed.

"Ugh, sniff, cough."

Y'know, I once read somewhere it is possible for a person to live off their excess fat. And, when there has been sporadic feedings this induces the chance of the condition's inception even more. Yeah. Since my cold's debut my appetite has decreased and the thought of ingesting my vile culinary concoctions pushes the urge to eat further back down the chain of 'to do' things daily. Hmm…

Leave the bathroom. Cross the kitchen. Enter the front room.

Sure there's a book on one of my shelves that will aptly assist in whipping the girl's growing girth away, leaving a model physique in its wakeful play. Which brings me to the glaring realization: Books have always been there for me.

I exit my place once more and return to the confines of my car.

Humans are mere mortal entities thus possessing many controlled as well as pronounced flaws. And, sometimes they cannot deliver or 'come through' due to either intended intentions or unforeseen phenomenal circumstance. Being that I am fastly a part of 21st Century humanity brood, I realize this as fact since sometimes I cannot even save myself from the everyday monetary misery and spiritual turmoil of adult life. And, for the most part, I happen to love me so, that's proof

Sick-n-Single (the breakdown)   55

positive we all as human beings harbor a genuine, internal 'Achille's heel.' When not monitored, this little piece of self-deception runs happily, expediently amok, creating an action of array filled with self-deception that some may never, ever recover from—thus inducing a stupefying, albeit relief from the actual reality they are not and will never truly experience life in the vein of genuine living and the pleasure of being alive—at least not in this incarnation of a lifetime.

Oops! While backing out the extra long driveway (amply covered with curling, sight reducing vine foliage) almost hit a jogger. Sure, it's raining. Actually, its been thundering and lightening. But, hey, people gotta stay fit. I hear ya.

Unlike most Northern Californian natives of my generation, I happen to love and appreciate Southern California. Jerk-a-linos and Jerk-a-linas be damned. The Water Wasters, coupled with the phony, fake, superficial Mammon worshipping citizens are a lot fewer than suspected or expected—when one dwells down here in the venerable Southland. Perhaps after the victorious Hetch Hetchy Dam incident from the 70s era, the majority of those soul challenged, empty individuals switched their Owner Occupied domiciles to other states. Let's say, Arizona, Nevada and even Oregon. "Hey, why not revive that illustrious senator, Mr. Barry Goldwater and his cult of ethics!" "Yucca Mountain, let's destroy!" "Wait 'til the rest of the lower 48 gets a hold of what we've done in otherwise quiet Or-ray-gun (for the other two states are not connected so do not count)!"

Whatever the case may be, it is my suspicion most of them cut. Left. Definitely split from this scene. Probably ending up in a lone star state working for energy companies in order to wreak more havoc upon the 49th acquirement of the U.S.A. Hmm…But, the praise of the southern portion of my home state region shall not be interrupted by mere manic memories from my childhood or grim, sordid recounts of the recent past. Southern California.

The weather, Jet Propulsion Lab, the opportunity, Caltech and overall aura of 'chance givers' makes it okay by me. Sure, NorCal has lots and SUPERlots to offer. Why San Francisco is the hometown of the greater Cal Tjader. Aaaaaah! Jazz alert, baby. That was a serious, serious music makin' human male. And, let's not forget, Levi's Jeans from the 1800s Goldminer Days got a popularly fast start there as well. Those mining '49ers. And, and, the ultimate yum, yum of American ice cream creations: the 'It's It.' The real San Francisco treat (after the 'fortune cookie'). (19)

The views, the fog (gotta clean that air), somebody's always thinkin', the cute guys, the bridges, the wowsie wow, wow intellect of both Stanford and U.C. Berkeley instructors, professors, students and graduate assistants combined, the true Constitution following constituency of Mendocino County (some say they print their own money, thank you!), the proximity to the Ocean, Bay and rivers, the wine country with all those lovely little spas-n-inns, and Yosemite National Park, hello Half Dome, will climb once again one day, the overall aura of 'oh yeah hep' that hippy power people left upon the region (firmly cementing with the Ohlone Indigenous Individuals before) Wow. Who in their right mind can deny San Francisco (and Greater Northern California for that matter) up to the early 1980s a place in their heart?

But, hey, why can't a girl fantasize a little? No Mr. Roarke and Tattoo, I do not need you. If I had it my way (y'know, like Mr. Sinatra) I'd simply purchase *The Incredible Mr. Limpet*, watch-n-study every detail then create my own personalized reality. Instead of the fish in the sea (with Lady Fish and all that strange bellowing yell-call), mine (my passage from this existence) would be either a book (at the top of the 'oh hell yeah' list of belonging on one's bookshelf). Most likely in the time of Hannibal Barca (with the general of course) or Egypt before it was known as Egypt and KMT for that matter. Not sure.

The competing fantasy land: Star Trek. A serious tug-of-war between the Original series and Voyager. Oh well. Unless I go completely mad or come across a serious wish giving genie, it ain't gonna happen.

Great sidenote that I know is a factual fact. Lucille Ball's Desilu Productions will always be cherished by me, the late Mr. Roddenberry and a tightly knit loyal fan base worldwide. Who says the L.A.P.D. can't produce something truly worthwhile and life changing in a most positive educational manner? Not me! And, not Desilu in 1966. However, the tripe which was imposed upon the same loyal band of space opera lovers needs to be thoroughly eradicated from any and all realms of existence. Enterprising not! What a bold, unsightly blemish you cast upon the rest of the greatest series ever broadcast!

All I can say, is the power of the page, will forever be my fortified stalwart wall of reliable, dependable structure. Those who came before, the powerfully particular specific individual adepts who were cut from the cloth of the brilliant genius material, left us words dictating ethics and structure to follow in order to perceive and achieve any obstacle we may or may not receive. Anyone failing due to reasons other than mental insanity or genetic physical incapability are truly the lazy and amply deserve to wallow in the wretched, wasteland of unfulfilled wonderment.

A resonating factor. Resolution.

About the only advantage brought forth from my illness is acquiring a depthness and baritone quality to my soft, high pitch voice. People take me more seriously when my vocal tonation is mired in reverberating depthness of pitch. However serious may be defined in these times.

My eyes casually slide by the popcorn section. For, I am now in *the store*. Was once told that in England people call corn, wheat. And, our corn "maize" or "Indian corn." I always wanted to know if popcorn was then called Popmaize or (A)maizin' Pop or perhaps Indian corn popped? Yes, the 'Creep-in.' Must refocus on…

"Cough. Cough."

A woman with a wandering toddler by her side, catches my eye. What had attracted my attention to them was her sudden snatching of the tot away from my direction. Yes, paranoia is everywhere.

It's the depth in tone and fright of catching "it." The unknown tainted venom known by me as a harmless cold but, when visited upon them can easily metamorphose into the new strain of the Marburg Virus. Ebola is everywhere! Okay. The advice of Chairman Mao himself resounds quite forcefully, "Be as shy as virgins and quick as rabbits."

Yep. A few more are scurrying away now as a deep rattle emerges from within my phlegm ravaged chest.

Hmm…isolation. Quiet time is to be had then. And, with sudden hushness comes stillness of outer thoughts. With this solitary removal from the noise pollution populous—memories, mixed with varied aspirations for the coming years spring forth.

As I ease into the 12 items or less line (at one point in time, I could've sworn it was "eight"), its length assures me I will have plenty of time to ruminate on this latest thought.

An abundance of knowledge of self is to be learned in this state of lullness. Sorta like the difference between 'enjoying life music' and 'gettin' shit accomplished' songs.

Case in point. Travelin' up the 5 north from Los Angeles to San Francisco via the Interstate 5 cuttin' over to the 152 (such a steep, angled right turn, man!) passin' through garlic Gilroy (after an initial hilly then willy nilly descent pass a majestic reservoir) in order to get to the 101 North. Why, only Donna Summer coupled with hardcore Heavy Metal (AC/DC (with Angus and Malcolm bangin' away at the guitars, how Young you were), Black Sabbath (old style), any Led Zeppelin (my fave, MUCHO arigatoo Jon Bonham, Jimmy Page, Robert Plant and John Paul Jones), the Cult (whom I will call by its real name forever *Death Cult* By the way, how are you doing, Mr. Peltier? Wish it could be a different, freer locale for you physically however the stars are just not right, everythings so topsy turvy. Nonetheless, back to the song-list, the Death Cult, okay Buffet & Astbury?), 80s era Madonna and the truly magnificent Rage Against the Machine (with the superHOT human being man, Zack de la Rocha hollerin' away)!!!!!!!

Yes, getting the drive over. Getting something accomplished.

In the region yearning to enjoy life? Well, how 'bout some John Coltrane? Let's begin with "Equinox." The middle includes the 'Acknowledgment' track from "A Love Supreme," along with "Central Park West," finishing with the majority of the versions he covered for Rodgers and Hammerstein's "My Favorite Things." Great side note.

When I traveled to Union Street from SFSU, on the 41 Union leg of my journey, it took 1 1/2 plays of the maiden voyage of Coltrane's rendition of "My Favorite Things" to make it to Union at Franklin. That is, if the damn electric bus poles didn't fall. If this occurred, I would call upon the assistance of David Bowie or if things really got outta control, Miles Davis.

Stan Getz! The Bossa Nova craze has never died in my world of one. It merely ebbs and flows to my particular preference. Chet Baker. Duke Ellington, any Cuban Danzon…Wes Montgomery (he of the gifted guitar), the surreal-n-clean Bach's "Air," Vivaldi, Patsy Cline's barely there steady plea for lovers to merely respect one another or better yet, reconcile, Led Zeppelin's "Rain Song," Cubanismo's "Danzon Daulena," Mongo Santamaria's "Together" and "Afro lypso" (very difficult to find since not to be had on compact disc only on vinyl and that's final!), "The Unforgettable Fire" of U2, "How deep is your love?" Thanks for asking Bee Gees, "La vie en Rose" from the great (little sparrow) Ediaf Piaf, Cesaria Evora (Cape Verde's own after Horace Silver) "Coragem Irmun," Virginie Rodrigues' "Negrume da Noite," Mr. George Michael: SUPERarigatoo for your exquisite pairing of "Cowboys and Angels," George Benson's "El Mar," Nat King Cole's "You call it madness (but I call it love)," Janis Joplin's rendition of "Trouble in Mind" and Lodi's own, Creedence Clearwater Revival's "Have you ever seen the rain?" Just to name a few.

Through our musical efforts of beauty, exquisite love and genuine artistic strives there can be plain, simple enlightenment. And, a most tantalizing enjoyment.

In closing, none other than the super, brilliant intellect of Robert S. de Ropp himself sufficiently suffices.

"It is a curious fact that the weaker the aspirant, the higher the demands he makes of his spiritual guide." (20)

And, the topper of the Topsters where profound proclamations proffered by the perished are concerned: "The practice of simple awareness is impossible without control of attention. Attention is to awareness as the oil in a lamp is to its flame…A man's level of consciousness can be measured by the freedom of his attention." (21)

He potently persists with, "We are caught up like flies in a spider's web, manipulated, directed, enchained. Look at the faces of people at the racetrack, a baseball game, a bullfight, a prizefight, any spectacle of a flamboyant or brutal kind. There is nothing behind the face. It is empty, a mask. The house is vacant.

"This is enslaved attention. In this condition, inner silence and simple awareness are lost and the whole field of consciousness is "occupied" by a victorious enemy...The name of the great enslaver is "Identification" and the result of his domination is "Waking Sleep." (22)

Oh and where did this highly accomplished, extremely well traveled biochemist (whom possessed a Ph.D. from the University of London as well as knew and considered great friends of Aldous Huxley, Charles Lindbergh, Timothy Leary, P.D. Ouspensky and Carlos Casteneda to name a few) choose to spend the remainder of his life before passing on? Why on a mountainside in Northern California. Hmm...ponder, ponder.

Now, with bag of 'over the counter' meds paid for and packed away. Bruised ego intact after suffering the intense scurrying afar and malevolent glares of death stares from the former fellow store patrons, back to the humble homestead I head.

"Ha chu."

"Bless you."

Wow, now, he's cute.

The last words spoken were neither from the sick-n-single narrator nor from her flu-beleaguered consciousness but, from a male stranger bestowing a wealth of care and concern upon his facial expression while holding the door open. No ring graces the ring finger. No tan line of one ever having been so is there either.

Inspired by HPL while pondering JPL

◆

shen brevard
Mel's Diner on Ventura Boulevard/Sherman Oaks fall 2004

Some crave normalcy or wish desperately to be immersed in the bland, vapid existence of the average day to day thoughts and activities of everyday Western (and depending on your proximity & location); Eastern, society. Acceptance. Where most humanity dwells is a mere creation of themselves—one massive mind "group think" founded, bounded and thoroughly reflected in the uncreative, unimaginative and hopelessly ignorant of what "living" truly conveys. To those willingly and unwillingly receiving the opportunity…who…witness the genuine spark of existing and evolving—the development can be providence (or simply put: dreadfully, deadfully fulfilling).

Grim glimpses of what could be, what should be, especially for me—a fairly attractive female. Unmarried. No STD's. No offspring. For the most part, in-shape. And, plenty of risqué to entertain the opposite sex. Yet, however, here I sit motionless, regretfully restrained to the passionless sidelines of life as various couples of differing preferences gloriously, vigorously engage in gregarious public displays of: Love. Affection. Tenderness. Lust. Words I know well by definition. Terms never used to describe any aspect of my three decade, plus, stint of existence thus far. My empty eyes emotionally seek salvation or a mere engrossing escape. Another scene is viewed.

The moon shimmers brightly while the stars are hidden by a thick veil of darkness harboring an absence of color rendering it so black, its void is thoroughly reminiscent of all the reinforced respect and common compassion so severely lacking in present day humanity.

The chatter, the careless (or is it carefree?) baseless conversations of the customers drag me back to reality. The here. The empty miasma of supreme mediocrity. The unbreathable incarnation of what is this physical manifestation that is so maligned with utter superficial, surface sincerity. Snippets, snatches and words are carelessly flung about then float my way. Vaunted degrees, cherished certificates and the super prestigious schools of academic excellence will soon tarnish and not matter when the Unnamable of mankind's distant past return. There are no more over-nourished forests. Systems will change, or rather, the values and importance bestowed upon them will simply dissolve into a deep (devouring) clinging nothingness. Unforeseen. Unthinkable. Upheaval. Word to the wise and most certainly unschooled: heed the utterings of the not so fictitious Ming the Merciless.

Watch what happens when we fling ourselves to places where we don't belong and simply do not, cannot comprehend. To tempt temptation or bask in self-glorification while blatantly ignoring our overall plight of inhumanity and self-inflicting cruelty can be a rapid recipe for a devastating comeuppance from those whose presence most of us simply refuse to acknowledge. Retribution will be a true collage of eerie esoteric ecstasy in reverse. The playing field of life no longer man's to define, malign or sideline. My appetite for anticipation neutrally (yet, mutually) awaits this manifestation.

Perdido in Flux (the quest)

◆

shen brevard
Beverly Hills Adjacent 1999/San Francisco 1999

J'ai peur...yo tengo temer...I fear. Love doesn't exist in fear. Can fear easily become engulfed by love or is it the other way around? A newborn desire embraces me with intermittent intentions well bred in lust. But, is lust ever pure? Furthermore, without the sanctity of goodness, what's to become of tempestuous passion? Regular life of bills and domicile and things to buy to live, keep us bound to work distracting and dismaying us from dalliances. In these places where we wish to be, promises of much more fruition coupled with a biting fate which creates a delectable strength bordering on the greatest enticement reigns.

In the light of the day, my thoughts only persist (or exist) in everlasting horizons where sunsets never cease. As both our ambitions intertwine and coax a rapture filled existence, tinged with a raucous rumba or a tempestuous tango, nothing more can be momentous. In this realm one gets lost in a drenching, quenching round of infinite ecstasy. As we explore one another in what could resemble a sensuous salsa or an intense samba, both (if not the latter moreso) embodied in nonstop desafinado: Ours is a union where only the light of the pale moon can temper hallowed titillation.

The marvelous, meticulous meandering of your tongue as it explores my soft body, supple to your touch...the same mouth caressing my ears with gentle words of embellishments...Do we comply with or condemn this wholehearted, anxious kinship? Or should we both retreat into our individual shells of protection seeking solace, the predictable and an eager desertion?

But why must we deny ourselves or banish each other to abject solitude, when we can both attain an obstinate enchantment? As the hours crawl by like a lazy, uninspired toddler, it is almost unbearable to think of just how many hours and seconds must be lived before my browns connect with your greens. For together, thus far, ours is a fleeting love. One that can only be housed in nothing more than a self-contained, torrentous augmentation of us as one. We create an energy so complete, so full that to encourage any words would cause an overflow into the unnecessary; rendering its whole purpose null and void. Upon achieving one of the many crests of delight, my consciousness is cast into a state of an uncontrollable omnipotent shaking revelation. Here, religion does not dwell. Where my senses now travel is in the land of the decadent divine. But with pure spirit comes qualified disdain.

J'ai perdu…Yo perdido…I have lost, I'm losing myself…my identity. As I discover myself, my inner, emotional boundaries (and the distant atavistic yearnings), the desire to seek, to join you explodes into a wholly, harrowing detail with exacting precision. Like a favorite photograph yellowing and fading with the passage of time: the charm is never touched, but the image simultaneously loses its freshness in the mind as it does in the tangible physical.

Is this latest ponderance just a rapid descent into the harrowing land of the perpetually concerned, or am I merely to wallow, to dissolve into a sweet, quiet whimper? One must always remember, no matter what voyage is established or road embarked upon: too much availability courts the unfulfilled mundane.

Bitter Thefts of Happiness

◆

shen brevard
Santa Monica spring 2002

Pick a time, choose a place but, if it is today, then be forewarned. For the land that dominates will be filled with arrogance abundant and humility in exile. Picture an individual. All this human being desires is the attainment of happiness and emotional enlightenment. This goal is to be achieved through writing. The conundrum, or rather what is becoming more of a solid complete obstacle, manifesting itself in low self-esteem, coupled with a teeming proliferance of indifferent, maniacal persons.

Seated solo at a table. Could be a house party or perhaps a mildly crowded bar. The thoughts of the individual turn and maneuver through a dense mental maze of malaise and frustration. A sense of spontaneity required to initiate a change, whether inside or outside, loosely encompasses the overall internal debate between mind, emotion and spirit.

When the thoughts are interpreted into words for all to see, below is the closest semblance to be.

To have a drink. To possess unquestionable friends. To mingle as they say. Socializing and existing as we should as living beings, it is not. Living that is. Being in the remote opposite atmosphere of healthy is the actuality. Hiding, shielding and basking in de-evolution in it's pure form is the reality. Present Day Society. Or, as it is said should be by greater society. However, who's society? Who comprises what defines and describes and composes "society?" What was before? What will be after? And, more importantly, what is it now?

To ponder or inquire such thoughts can only lead to a road divided into two extremes; sane and insane. Either route leads to loss. Whether mind or popularity among the masses (or their thoughts), depends on the one who observes the query or situation. Noncommittal is the theme of the day. Or, is it instability? Mediocrity is disguised as a mass illness of mental decrepitude while nostalgia is religiously propagated as the guaranteed cure. This, however, is only what can be described as a temporary "fix." And, this is attempted by a minimal, few. Long-term effective remedy and alleviation can uniquely and ultimately be attained by the age old, genuine slayer of the wronged…love.

Doubling as the first defense against the deranged, love is the last bastion of greatness; the true apex of humanity…even as other fortitudes of strength, greatness and goodness are being infinitesimally dissolved daily. While respect for fellow man is savagely ravaged relentlessly, love remains as yet touched by the superficially trite, arrogant and ignorantly selfish. But not for eternity will this be. Unfortunately for organic's sake, it's barrier possesses borders which can tear. You wonder if the borders are coming undone?

Only look, feel the anxious, eager iniquity permeating the very fabric of the atmosphere of the now, the today. Why all the suffering? Why numerous invocations of morally injustices? The blatantly powerful overpowering the shamelessly powerless; especially in the meager domiciles of the struggling lands of ancient Gondwanaland. Hmm…No individual is thoroughly Innocent and Just while none deserves the perilous injustice and demonic treachery being perpetrated upon so many innocent and too many young right at this instance as you read these words and curiously while it is being written in this form. Why?

It is believed throughout the course of humanity, a sort of justice, a faint shadow of a great cosmic yin yang, will balance everything. Thus, the Wronged, will be justified if not now, then later. When is later? More importantly, will "later" ever materialize? Those who pose as champions of the underdogs will be exposed as fraudulent and divinely punished. But will they really? "They" is a word fit to describe those who maim and render all hope, fairness and happiness lame. No genuine maltreatment is ever televised or known by the majority. Only sound bytes of fabrications that really serve to enslave the populace further exists. More like persists. Remember. Please remember and don't forget.

Your very humanity relies on what is internally embedded and understood but is always manipulated until forgotten and unknown by the persuasive external ungood. Those who populate the very den of gross deception fair only slightly better due to a bit more insight courtesy of their malicious deeds. Is there a day on the bleak horizon of the inhumane deeds of today; where "They" are to halt or be halted? And, if so, will the persecuted witness the prosecution of their villainous violators?

Who will be the prosecutor of the maniacally inclined in the arena of power, authority and economic servitude? Ponderings and wonderings seem to only multiply as of late while viciousness feverishly procreates among the spiritual dwellings of the mentally weak and horribly, physically and materially impoverished. Something is on the horizon. I know. Something is stirring and yearns to be heard and known by all. Whether it's the final apocalyptic *Just* here to serve the everlasting fire to the damned and wicked—I do not know. Or, perhaps it's purpose is to enforce only more draconian thefts of happiness? Whichever face is displayed, whatever actions define the player, just remember, only remember with a true heart, justice is a word transversing barriers of existence while the balance of power for all that IS and what will ever BE in this universe is vengeance. Just remember that.

Random Ring

◆

shen brevard
Beverlywood bungalow spring 2005

Lying in bed on a late Saturday morning. Body lounging while thoughts lingering. "What to do today?

"Tasks as in clothes washing, grocery shopping, light bathroom cleaning, a meandering park stroll, reorganizing bills on the cluttered kitchen counter top…or nothing? Hmm…just lie and be lazy. Don't even need a couch to be a potato. I prefer the 'lazy lima bean' epithet.

"Sounds cuter. Potatoes can look rough. Hmm…perhaps I'll fire up the gas guzzler and journey to the edge of West Hollywood in order to purchase a classic DVD or two? A Lana Turner picture show or a Godzilla all out monster bashin' beatdown? Megalon, here I come! Hey, gots the popcorn and wine already. Of course will wait 'til darkness falls. Films such as the aforementioned are best viewed after the sun with its infernal light no longer hangs in the sky.

"Now, this is sounding better and bet…"

The burgeoning idea-plan ends as a single, solitary squeal of a ringing telephone pierces the quiet of the semi-disheveled bedroom. The girl, still on her back, atop her bed, while eyeing her canopy, slowly sits up. Her eyes locate the cordless phone.

All sound ceases. Curious, she goes to the phone and looks upon its face (e.g. the caller i.d. unit).

"Reifman, G. Hmm…who might you be?"

She replaces the cordless back upon its recharger as her mind conjures various conjectures and scenarios of the unknown G. Reifman.

"Perhaps a young guy. Not too bad looking but, far from the handsome. Mere victim of a nightclub number misdirect. But, wait, he only let it ring once thus was probably aware of the err in dialing. Or, too shy and withdrawn. Couldn't find the words…"

She lies back down—this time on her side allowing one leg to slowly dangle back and forth off the side of the bed. Her arms are carelessly flopped above her head.

"He could be older. Hmm…explaining the one ring correction. Yeah, 70-ish. I can see the grayish hair now. Short cut, neat and trim style. Light prescription glasses covering squinting eyes. Hand shaking just a bit but able to keep the phone receiver steady. Voice proclaiming, 'Eh, that's not the number.'

"A soft, audible click on his end. A single whine on mine. What did he have for breakfast? Maybe he was calling to order some? Nah. He probably drinks Ensure. Hmm…however G. Reifman could be young or youngish.

"Let's say late 30s, early 40s. This version of G.R. misdialed out of anger. Yeah. This age range harbors a lot of tension these days. Don't I know it."

The girl switches sides and allows her other leg to now hang just above the hardwood floor—swinging to and fro.

"He was callin' his mechanic, 'Why the fuck isn't my car ready yet, dammit!'

"The accident had been his fault but, hey, that's why people have car insurance. And, y'know G. R. has full coverage. 'Growl!' Yeah, there he was just yesterday, his harried stressed out car insurance agent nervously on the phone informing him, 'Greg, this is it, I'm sorry that's the sixth accident you've caused in six months. We can no longer carry your policy.'

"Greg R. hollerin' back, 'They were justifiable causes. Every single damn one of them! You should see the raving lunatics they allow out on the streets these days!' The agent quietly responding with, 'I know.'

"The call ends. G.R. is livid pissed. He has one more payment due on his now canceled policy. Instead of not paying thus unleashing the relentless wrath of credit hobgoblins upon his 767 fico score, he writes a check. And, in bright red permanent marker scrawls upon the face of the detachment included with the bill, 'KISS MY ASS!!!!'

"Poor guy's so out of it, can't even remember his mechanic's number. Callin' me instead. While I'm in bed."

The girl chuckles and sits up.

"Man, I'm even a little heated now. His policy shouldn't be canceled because of cracker jack box driver's license holding people. I've seen a few of them non-drivin' cats out there scootin'' around through traffic raising all sorts of hellish havoc. It ain't pretty. Hmm…"

She sits upon the edge of the twisted sheets and tangled comforter. Her visual attention falls upon her wardrobe while the mysterious G. Reifman continues to dominate her mental processes.

"What if he *was* intentionally calling me? Yeah. He saw me while I was at a stop light in the magnificent muscle car. Just being Californian. No stare of standoffishness, no arrogance, no mean muggin' was I. Just *all cool with it* aura. Uh huh.

"Jotted down the license plate number and embarked upon the search for the mysterious muscle car maiden. Once proper telephone number attained, he eagerly awaited for the next Saturday morning to come around. 'Must not call too early nor too late.' The day arrived. Why, today. He dialed the number then abruptly hung up.

'Bitch could have problems.' "Hmm…a misogynist. Glad he didn't follow through. Or, he does not take the chicken out route.

"A date is made and kept. He shows up drivin' a rare white Ranchero—pristine with a nicely waxed sheen. We go to the beach then to bed. Strange how more protection is avidly sought from UV rays.

"Ah, my precious little crumb snatcher, Daddy drove a white Ranchero. You don't see too many of either around these days. Hah, hey maybe the missing Dadas are driving the elusive makes down hidden roads and little lost lanes?

"Ewh, this fantasy isn't cute at all! More like a fantastic nightmare. Oh, G.R. such a harrowing psychological vacuum you have wrought!"

The girl releases a giggle.

"Jeez, guess who has no life?"

She stands, stretches then begins to separate her white colored clothing from her nonwhite colored clothing.

"But, at least I have an imagination. Wonder if G. Reifman does too? Hey, what if G. Reifman is a woman? Oh well…Later on this eve it shall be Mothra-n-me doing the Gojira deed. Per chance, even the "Naruto" clan (with my fave Gaara) joining the Saturday night entertainment steed. (23)

Mendicant Exceptionelle (psalmody)

◆

shen brevard
Los Angeles (Marina del Rey) spring 2005

Calling in sick when not sick but, hoping to use a sick day instead. Hmm…Hump day. Wednesday. The middle of the work week, for the average Citizen Ordinary. However, suppose, just imagine for one delicious little second, there is a particularly savvy individual possessing a slightly more enhanced vision and harboring a keen comprehension as to the real undercurrent of modern society's indiscreet undermining underpinning mechanism and influential environment. The often theorized but now revived, subtle soul kill.

Ah, Ouspensky, how true you are as is de Ropp. "Man is a prisoner of his own lies. If he knows the truth the truth will set him free." (24)

Grim, crooked social mores to animal feebleness and of course the profusely prevalent deviant human forays. This particular poised, potent person snaps loose from the mundane and meticulously meanders effortlessly into the SUPERaware fantastic—in order to formulate a most glorious report.

From desk jockeys to dirt bags, homemakers to hooligans, unfortunate schmoos thrown in jail (the dreaded incarceration) for no reason (left to rot) to flesh possessing folks who ought not be allowed to participate within 21st Century's international playpen. No, no no little Timmy should never have been permitted to come out and play. For now as the rest of us may say, "We've gotta putrid, permanent pig sty!"

Tell Mommie-n-Daddie but, uh right now they're just too high. Drugs, booze but wait now it's the patriotic religious smooze. Hmm…Independent thought has ventured so horribly astray since that very first Independence Day. Jeepers, Mr. Ben Franklin. Good Golly, General Washington! Oh m'gosh, Ambassador Jefferson! Hey to ya, Hamilton. Goddammit, Mr. George Mason! Your insightful, rightful intentions have been foolishly flung into a lost-n-found bin with a bottomless pit. My whole take on democracy? Always fight for something not necessarily you thoroughly, totally believe in, as the 'just right,' and 'dead on' center of good. This ploy severely alleviates damning disappointment. Anything man makes with a mortal mind is flawed. So, one seems most wise to wait until a replacement, a resounding resolution can be had before eradicating the current bad.

If not followed up by a justly fulfilling prop-up, the vacuum that is instigated could probably prove worse than the initial zealous mayhem. Then what an intensely long mop up whose end may or may not ever present itself. And, who is going to volunteer for this most inglorious, tedious of the tiresome gig? Not me.

For y'see, the problem's the bullets the solution's the bucks. Lifestyle and moving, domicile and dictating stagnation. Let's just keep it up to snuff. Only those who truly dare to live life shall survive. And, within that minute proportion of the said populous, still rare shall there exist those who are to possess the sheer essence of exigent, undoubted happiness. This is something monetary exchange can neither guarantee nor attain.

To continue with the eloquent explique of the joys and woes of living below paycheck to paycheck: Viva Vagabondia! And not even a calm inducing Slavic Daino to ease or soothe the fragmented nerves! To stand forthright in a position of self-determination while life provides the parade of faces who mostly pass yet some do cling (family, as in relatives, kinda don't count in most cases, they will, for the most part be there regardless e.g. the funeral, family reunion, wedding circuit approach).

Self-evolution and courtin' its magnificent manifestation into personal existence can be one big bang up drag—brimming with an angst filled penetrating isolation. And, unremember not, satisfaction or any resulting stimulation is guaranteed non!

Paging a necessary segue so the Mendicant will have one less qualifier to satisfy. Oh my. None found so, hope the tepid turbulence of the transition is not too 'read no more' tempting. Ya gotta stick around.

Nearby street activity sounds provide more subject for fodder. A car sputters then dies. It is a foreign make. Surprise. Surprise. I guess things such as this can happen. So much for Bavarian (or is it German?), know how. But the Scandinavians—now—they run a tight, efficient ship. And, unbeknownst to all in the world (save for a few), a Norwegian second mate of the two-masted schooner 'Emma' (from Auckland), a certain Gustaf Johansen, once saved the world from an entirely wretchedly bad fate.

When the stars were right, he slayed the malevolent incarnate with a most bodacious rammin' jammin' action. Like a persistent car salesman plying innocent people into pretty cars with ugly innards.

My manager's American made vehicle along with its constitution of connivances is brought to the forefront of my thoughts.

The manner in which the manager's auto's internal computer had to be reset in order to offset a "miniature" malfunction—that's what I desire for my current conscious path: "Can I getta reset, please?!" Pass along a healthy dose of scintillating ignorance just for kicks. But, this process will most likely fail—sputter and cease to cease. Like my manager's car dubbed, Fritz.

Around since the '20s (the manufacturer not the make), what if something otherworldly sinister lies behind the infamously behemoth car company? Say an alien entity infernally bent on the silent slaughter of the human race as we understand it. Their motto throughout the millennia when things became a bit too boisterous for their liking: "Time for a trimmin'."

The Great Magnetic pole shift. The sudden extinction of the dinosaurs. Noah's flood. Kilauea. Pompeii. And of course, the Christian prophetic prose of the 'Fire Next Time.' Watch out for entities named Henry.

Hey Gustaf Johansen! I believe your heroic services are required once more. (25)

Now, talk about a most licentious extraction of lipo regarding people. March 2006 could bring a burstin' purse for Persians possessin' Bourse. My sentiment: unlikely. Trim, trim. Snip, snip. Terror here, an' terror there. Why, we sell terror everywhere. Whomever so comprises the We or US momentarily. Yes they dare create monstrous chaotic havoc within their very own lairs. Oh devil may care! Must collect that gross share of the petrol and natural resource fare. Dwindle, dwindle, swindle. Life just ain't fair.

Just ask all those who precariously slipped to their deaths off South African chairs. Guatemalan politicians circa 1954, bend that ear, loud an' clear. Stalin fave, depraved Ukrainians, Georgians during the heyday of Mr. Cocktail (the Vyacheslav). Nationality is the new King "Ism."

Guess who's back at it? Gregariously sprouting forth verbose vacuity fastly attached to deceptive yet effective enthralling diversions. Oh yeah. Serving as a two-for-one descript, it can apply to the strangely out-of-tune entertainment industry of the 21st Century. Ahem, Horror Flicks set to, what? PG-13 tune. A bit more on that dangerous yet sad desafinado later. Much later perhaps. For y'see some things are eagerly revamped, rehashed then revised with the concluding result reflecting a sorry finish. Other institutes and brands just never seem to undergo unnecessary 'improvement' or blandly orchestrated change.

The said car company from the dawn of the previous century, to this very vernal day in the fifth year of the 21st century, that stalwart, manages to survive since a sorta sentimental pride etched upon the cosmic conscious psyche of the patriots of the land intrinsically persists, "It must never ever perish, lest we ourselves are in the throes of extinction, dang it!"

Sadly for them, they go about blissfully unaware their steadfastly, stubborn dogma maintaining an historick societal fixture alive sadistically seals their very own fatal demise.

"Time for a trimmin'."

A most dapper, daring gentleman hailing from 1900s Rhode Island put it best (August 20, 1890 was an authentically beautiful summer day indeed!), *"Commercialism and decent literature have no meeting-point except by accident."*

"Literature cannot be forced. Nothing really worth reading was ever deliberately or intentionally—or even wholly consciously—written. Art is not what one resolves to say, but what insists on saying itself through one. It has nothing to do with commerce, editorial demand, or popular approval. The only elements concerned are the artist and the emotions working within him." (26)

This cannot be said of the movies of today as of the very recent time era. The horror genre has been most consistently inflicted upon as of late. To get horror right there can be no horror-lite. Diet does not always render the best results. Like a drama without conflict. Sci-Fi with no science. And, Winnie the Pooh with no honey or baby Roo. Can anyone imagine Swift's Gulliver afraid to travel? Or, my fave, Diet Tab. Was there ever such a thing?

Creativity is what it's all about. Take for instance having Fred Williamson as 'Black Caesar' dying on H.P. Lovecraft's 'would have been' birthday (circa 1972). And, by the way, that has got to hold the record for the longest active 'dying' (scene) sequence put onto film. Inference makes it all go swimmingly. And, no gratuitous sex, please! Why not wanton talent? The floodgates should overflow with wondrous wordplay and dazzling displays of acting sorties. If ya just don't get it, then, leave this category alone, please. Find something else to render mediocre.

But alas until this has come to pass, suffer the audience must. There are even rumors of films begin shot without written scripts! Norma Desmond is their patron saint, for reals! Who needs mouths when glitzy marketing budgets are possessed and better still, solid product placement fund actors who sleepwalk through rehashed, semi-thought out symbols not even found on paper. Talk about non de script.

To the densely surprised, even the audience is catching on to the flim flam sham. Who's gonna show up for the dullest dulling looksey in town? What's a studio, an actor, a stylist and crew to do? The balance of good should kick in one day. There is always that off brand chance Burt Lancaster's 'Valdez' is coming. And upon his ceremonious arrival all that is wrong and so horribly askew concerning cinema reels, motion picture shows, its business and quality work they all feverishly eschew will be put back just right. Nice-n-tight, thank you.

When it all comes down to it. When the words, the shouts, the cries, the sarcastic gripes and perjured moans have climaxed then diminished, what awaits US at the finished finales? When the towel is thrown in, don't, I repeat do not, expect much. When most cling to unexceptional diversions as opposed to existence validating excursions, the topsy turvy prevails and all life is truly a living, waking hell.

Personally, taking a chance against sadistic, fiendishly secretive space brothers lingering in a dimension just the next existence over is my secret fantasy 'brass ring.' At least some kinda benevolently divine intervention may present itself and prevail. Here's that second chance and rose garden all at once not just a sorry, sour sucker punch.

A sorta natural order of the cosmic, galactic kind. The secret, powerfully illustrious ally protectively bellowing, "Pick on someone within your own vibrational frequency, Thog! For these clueless clogs are doing just fine performing the cultivation of a most perfect suicide vine."

But reality wise, the best way to survive, thus triumphantly overcome this present banal, vapid, physical state is through employing P.D. Ouspensky's fourth way, that of the Sly Man. In this guise, "one was smart enough to drink with the Devil and leave the Devil to pay for the drinks."

Always utilize every situation in life to your advantage. No matter how coarse or inconvenient things may become. It's the reaction to the situation. Not the action of the circumstance's existence of being that is the ultimate fate determiner.

Now one modern, monetarily challenged Mendicant must see about setting her bank account to reflect just that. For on my knees I shall not be. Unless I desire—that's the key.

Blue Bay Arean Bye-Cha

◆

shen brevard
Los Angeles summer 1999

every once in a while when things go awry and i just might want to cry, and giving up seems the most achievable and conceivable, something from within, not from deep but maybe just near the surface of my hopes, dreams and wishes; lets me know tomorrow may just bring what yesterday didn't and today wouldn't possibly consider.

to be at peace doesn't sound like the impossible feat it has become today. however, as the ticking of the clock determining the existence of all nature's creatures continues, and time forages onward; man and woman, who together compose humanity, are really just waiting in an invisible realm. awaiting something that can either be termed "the horrid," or "the fantastic."

at times i wonder why i allow my surroundings to remain as unkempt as the misconstrued ideas and fantasies which wile away time in my abstract subconscious mind. almost always is the sweet, exquisite taste of make-believe just at the tip of my anxious fingertips. almost forever is my brooding depression anxiously awaiting to remind me of reality and all its brutal consequences and outright injustices inflicted upon the good and perpetuated by the bad. almost never is a resolution achieved or conclusion attained.

evil and sweet. mischievous and coy. who or what defines pleasure and pain? there is a point where the two do blur; whether physical or surreal, fact or imagined. if i held a knife in my hand, would i be ending or beginning a life? if the same utensil were held by the same hands and a cake were the object of its purpose; would that be a celebration of rebirth as well? if an oven were added to the scenario and there was no food to cook but, only food for thought, which metaphorically had grown stale, bad and tasteless. the food for thought would be placed in the preheated oven and simply bake away, cook away and best of all burn away and kill the soured hope and spoiled dreams.

but, as sordid as these words may appear, my thoughts are not as drenched in succulent dread as one may perceive. for some reason, from some place, something just over the horizon of indescribable pleasure beckons me to continue. more than hope and just shy of the wonderful ultimate; this elusive variable, this apparition is definable and not, all at once. simultaneous duality's of confusion, eagerness, dread, impatience and abundance ebbs forward and sideways and any other direction where my mind is the indirect target.

in a time where most can no longer have their own lives as theirs, where only a few control so many, where destinies are only for those who show and act upon selfish disdain; i believe if only a simple little wish of mine could be attained, i wouldn't depend, need or court the undefinable thing just over my mental horizon being.

fog. plain and simple. clear and cool, gray and clean. to bask in its presence is like being cleansed from the inside out. to stop the ever present daily barrage of the hot, angry sun with its relentless rays of aging destruction is what this cover from the sky achieves, attains. at the end of the day is just the beginning for sheer, clean pleasure for most when the fog rolls in off the calm and serene north pacific. as a quote goes, "it touches everything but leaves everything unchanged." (27) to be in its range of beckoning is my most specific plan to battling the long, hot days of southern california.

to sell yourself (or really is it just your ideas?) in order to move back to a place where you moved away from. why does success seem to have a boomerang quality? if one "makes" it in their field; and truly does break from the mass-man in order to etch out a personal, self-defined lifestyle; will the urge to return, to retrace your path to your "home" of your youth, with all its safe, familiar qualities ever leave one alone? does the nagging hometown simply drift asunder as the newly victorious individual basks, gloats and takes hold of their hard earned glory? i'm not sure. but perhaps when something sells, i'll experience that path.

"Man is something to be surpassed. What have you done to surpass man?"

Friedrich Nietzsche's *Zarathustra*

Notes and Bibliography

1. Actual phrase-moniker coined by H. Lee in Greenwich Village, New York City (circa 1998).

2. Gardner, Ava. *Ava My Story* (New York: Bantam Books, November 1990). Ms. Gardner knew of this as she was gifted with such a jewel by an utterly enamored Mr. Howard Hughes.

3. Three versions of the Japanese bullet train exist. Listed by speed classification: Nozumi, Hikari and Kodama. The last being the 'slowest' and according to a random conversation-mate in Tokyo, is to be decommissioned. Hasn't happened yet, though.

4. Alas, this curious positioning has fallen by the wayside. In 2004, one could amply observe these two genres together. Now, it is slowly being phased out in most bookstores across this nation.

5. A definite recommend for late afternoon/early evening casual motoring jaunt on this fabulously circuitous famed Southland thoroughfare.

6. Lovecraft, H.P. *The Best of H.P. Lovecraft (Bloodcurdling Tales of Horror and the Macabre/The Call of Cthulhu)* (New York: The Random House Publishing Group, 1963).

7. Rux, Bruce. *Architects of the Underworld, Unriddling Atlantis, Anomalies of Mars, and the Mystery of the Sphinx* (Berkeley, California: Frog, Ltd. North Atlantic Books,1996). Incredibly talented fact divulging individual. Never a dull rendition of information transmission. Always mind twisting.

7a. Rux, Bruce. *Hollywood Vs. the Aliens. The Motion Picture Industry's Participation in UFO Disinformation* (Berkeley, California: Frog, Ltd. North Atlantic Books, 1997). Yet another tantalizing tome both entertaining and cerebrally engaging.

8. Lovecraft, H.P. *The Transition of H.P. Lovecraft: The Road to Madness (At the Mountains of Madness)* (New York: Ballantine Books by arrangement with Arkham House Publishers, Inc, October 1996).

9. Boyd, Doug. *Rolling Thunder* (New York: Dell Publishing Co., Inc., 1974). This in-depth study of the life of a Western Shoshone Shaman is a must for providing an acute introspection of the blatant chaining of pinyon trees in the western region of the U.S. circa 1970s. As well as an interesting, unbiased look into Rolling Thunder's approach to life as a 'teacher' through example regarding man's overall power if lived in harmony coupled with respect concerning nature and all living creatures. Interesting side note: Tom Laughlin (of 'Billy Jack' celluloid fame) included Rolling Thunder on film (divulging pertinent information in the Shoshone language). Arigatoo, Mr. Laughlin for the visual and verbal exposure.

10. Lovecraft. H.P. *The Transition of H.P. Lovecraft: The Road to Madness (At the Mountains of Madness)* (New York: Ballantine Books by arrangement with Arkham House Publishers, Inc, October 1996).

11. De Ropp, Robert S. *Warrior's Way: The Challenging Life Games* (New York: A Merloyd Lawrence Book Published by Delacorte Press/Seymour Lawrence, 1979/reprinted 1984 by arrangement with Delacorte Press).

12. Actually hard liquor may induce a speedier acceleration to brain cell death. Wine, perhaps takes a bit longer. Although, the cheaper the grade, a gray area is entered. Just my own homegrown assumption so, not exactly sure of this as validity.

13. Greenburg, Stanley R. (screenplay by)/Harrison, Harry (based upon book by), *Soylent Green* (motion picture,1973). In truth, it was neither. Mr. van Patten's brief appearance was merely as an usher—who by the way—was semi-roughed up by cynically, quasi corrupt hero Detective Thorn (brilliantly portrayed 'camp style' by Mr. Charlton Heston).

14. Jaffe, Robert and Jaffe Steven-Charles (written by), *Motel Hell* (motion picture, 1980). A phrase made popular by Wolfman Jack in this cult classic. Super Side Note: if purchasing said DVD, make sure to attain the double feature paired

with *Deranged* (motion picture, 1974) Ormsby, Alan (written by). Roberts Blossom portrayal of Ezra Cobb (the butcher of Woodside!) along with his classic horror style 'semi-dead' mother is a Horror Head MUST OWN!!! From the death scene at the inception, off the wall (in your face) antics, the craggily commentator and straight out, directly off brand dialogue, one can only help but be thoroughly entertained.

15. De Ropp, Robert S. *Warrior's Way: The Challenging Life Games* (New York: A Merloyd Lawrence Book Published by Delacorte Press/Seymour Lawrence, 1979/reprinted 1984 by arrangement with Delacorte Press).

16. Strange as it may seem, even after the 38 Geary line acquired the double stretch coaches, the operators of this route continued with the deliberate 'pass up.' Some seem to even *floor it* as an angered confusement mounted on the should have been passengers' visages.

17. Again, the passage of time has rendered yet another cherished memory to a sorta revamping. No longer monthly, the Fort Mason branch is now open Saturday and Sunday. And, there's even a permanent bookstore within the confines of the San Francisco's Main Public Library on Larkin Street. No view of Crissy Field or nature there. I guarantee that. Only the 19 Polk MUNI bus along with the 5 Fulton line and depending on your angle of stance, San Francisco City Hall. Which, mind you, was designed as a replica of Les Invalides in Paris, France. The burial chamber of Napoleon Bonaparte. Exclusivity is a rapidly fading trend of the past.

18. Leith, W. Compton. *Serenica* (Portland, Me.: Printed for Thomas Bird Mosher, 1927).

19. If one desires a true deluge of California history, please be my guest and check out both Kevin Starr's *Americans and the California Dream 1850-1915* (1973). Plus, *City of Quartz* by Mike-you're-so-brilliant-Davis (1990). And, top these two choices off with *California Gold Days*, Helen Bauer's 1957 account in the California State Series collection. Positively sure more volumes exists which divulge even more pertinent historical information. However, this is a sure fire initiation into dazzling Cali-factoids. Guaranteed to impress family, friends and casual discussion-mate.

20. De Ropp, Robert S. *The Master Game: Pathways to Higher Consciousness beyond the Drug Experience* (New York: "A Delta/Seymour Lawrence book" Originally published by Dell, 1989).

21. ibid.

22. ibid.

23. Simply put: one of the greatest anime series created (and that's including Matsumoto Leiji's *Galaxy Express 999* and Carl Macek's revamped *Robotech* series). Even though Naruto is the 'star' ninja-in-training, Gaara of the Sand Village is totally bad-ass! With Lee Rock and the three legendary ninjas (Tsunade-sama, Ochimaru-sama and Jiraiya-sama) included high on the list of the best as well. Come to think of it, the entire Konoha and Sand village ninjas pretty much hold their own with their specialized techniques and powers. In order to get the full, mesmerizing effect, must view in native Japanese language with English subtitles.

24. De Ropp, Robert S. *The Master Game: Pathways to Higher Consciousness beyond the Drug Experience* (New York: "A Delta/Seymour Lawrence book" Originally published by Dell, 1989).

25. Not to spoil anything but, kinda difficult if one does read H.P. Lovecraft's astounding *The Call of Cthulhu* and realize Mr. Johanssen's outcome. Oh well. It's fiction, right?

26. Lovecraft, H.P./edited by Joshi, S.T. and Schultz, David E. *Lord of a Visible World: An autobiography in Letters* (Athens, Ohio: Ohio University Press. 2000).

27, Not sure if this was verbally or visually attained. I must admit my reading throughout the years, at times, intertwines with spoken information with various conversation-mates. However, if pressed, I would give this credit to the late, great Dr. Robert S. de Ropp (visually) passed along to me.

Addendum: in regards to Robert S. de Ropp, other books not mentioned but, makes interesting reading:

Self-Completion: Keys to the Meaningful Life
Sex Energy
The New Prometheans
Church of the Earth
Eco-Tech
Drugs and the Mind
Man Against Aging
Science and Salvation

Another author's material worth acquiring: R.A. Schwaller de Lubicz. Deliciously fascinating factoids (and life elevating elements) are sure to be appeasingly revealed while instilling a new outlook upon sustaining a fulfilling life.

The Temple in Man: Sacred Architecture and the Perfect Man
A Study of Numbers: A Guide to the Constant Creation of the Universe
Esoterism and Symbol
Sacred Science: The King of Pharaonic Theocracy

978-0-595-37185-3
0-595-37185-X

Printed in the United States
43673LVS00007B/67